A Calendar of Country Customs

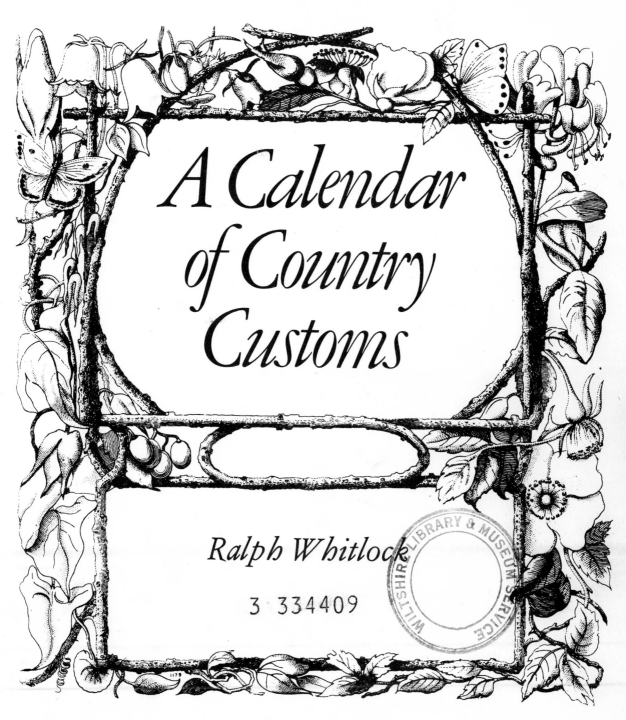

A Calendar of Country Customs

Ralph Whitlock

B. T. BATSFORD LTD.
London

First published 1978
Copyright Ralph Whitlock 1978
ISBN 0 7134 0571 6
Typeset by Tek-Art Ltd. in Garamond, 10 on 13pt
Printed by Cox & Wyman Ltd, Fakenham, Norfolk
for the Publishers B. T. Batsford Ltd,
4 Fitzhardinge Street, London W1H 0AH

Contents

Illustrations

Short Bibliography

Armstrong, Edward A. *The Folklore of Birds*, 1958
Boase, Wendy *The Folklore of Hampshire*, 1976
Boyd, A.W. *A Country Parish*, 1950
Brand, J. *Observations on Popular Antiquities*, 1900
Briggs, Katharine M. *The Folklore of the Cotswolds*, 1974
Chambers' Book of Days, 1864
Deane Tony & Shaw, Tony *The Folklore of Cornwall*, 1975
Evans, George Ewart *The Horse in the Furrow*, 1954
Evans, George Ewart *Ask the Fellows who make the Hay*, 1956
Field, Rev. J.E. *The Myth of the Pent Cuckoo*, 1913
Hampshire Federation of Women's Institutes *It Happened in Hampshire*, 1937
Harris, J. Rendel *The Origin & Meaning of Apple Cults*, 1919
Hole, Christina *English Custom & Usage*, 1940
Hole, Christina *English Traditional Customs*, 1975
Jones-Baker, Doris *The Folklore of Hertfordshire*, 1977
Killip, Margaret *The Folklore of the Isle of Man*, 1975
Kingston, Francis *Fragments of Two Centuries*, 1893
Marwick, Ernest *The Folklore of the Orkneys & Shetlands*, 1975
Olivier, Edith *Moonrakings*, 1930
Palmer, Kingsley *The Folklore of Somerset*, 1976
Palmer, Roy *The Folklore of Warwickshire*, 1976
Patten, R.W. *Exmoor Custom & Song*, 1974
Porter, Enid *Cambridgeshire Customs & Folklore*, 1969
Porter, Enid *The Folklore of East Anglia*, 1974
Readers' Digest *Folklore, Myths & Legends of Britain*, 1973
Ross, Anne *The Folklore of the Scottish Highlands*, 1976
Rowling, Marjorie *The Folklore of the Lake District*, 1976
Simpson, Jacqueline *The Folklore of Sussex*, 1973
Simpson, Jacqueline *The Folklore of the Welsh Border*, 1976
Tongue, R. & Briggs, K.M. *Somerset Folklore*, 1965
Tyzack, Rev. G. *The Lore & Legend of the English Church*, 1899
Whitcombe, Mrs. H.P. *Bygone Days in Devon & Cornwall*, 1875
Whitlock, Ralph *A Family & a Village*, 1969
Whitlock, Ralph *The Folklore of Wiltshire*, 1976
Whitlock, Ralph *The Folklore of Devon*, 1977

Acknowledgements

The author and publishers would like to thank the following for permission to reproduce the illustrations in this book: Birmingham Public Library no. 25, (Benjamin Stone Collection) no. 15; Central Press Photos nos 10, 34; Exeter City Library no. 18; Fox Photos nos 7, 14, 17, 22, 26, 33; The Jainer Collection no. 12; Keystone no. 3; Leicester Evening Mail no. 6; Museum of English Rural Life, Reading University nos 24, 29; Museum of Lakeland Life and Industry, Kendal no. 27; Oxford City Library no. 13; Sport and General no. 1; F.R. Winstone no. 21. The author would like to record his grateful appreciation of all the help and co-operation given by the staff of Yeovil Library.

Introduction

THE LIFE of our ancestors had for its horizons the hedges of the village fields. In those fields they ploughed and hoed and harvested. Along the village lanes they drove their cows and sheep to pasture. In the woods they gathered nuts and firewood and set their pigs foraging for acorns. On the moors and downs beyond the limits of cultivation they watched their sheep grazing through the short summer months.

Because they had no artificial illumination, other than candles or rush-lights, they went to bed early and rose early. Working hours, except at the height of summer, were from sunrise to sunset, or in some instances from half-an-hour before sunrise to half-an-hour after sunset. Sunday was a holiday, but everyone was expected to attend church. There was, indeed, nowhere else to go.

Once or twice a year, perhaps, the villagers would walk to the nearest town, several miles away. Their visits would generally coincide with a fair. But many villagers did not get even that break from routine. In the 1820s William Cobbett met in a village near Andover a young woman aged between 20 and 30 who had never ventured more than two-and-a-half miles from the cottage where she was born.

Confined within such narrow limits, they had to find their pleasure in the context of their programme of work. Fortunately, the cycle of farm life produces its own natural seasons for festivity. Seedtime and harvest come round as regularly as day and night. So, too, do hay-making, sheep-shearing, the mating of sheep, the autumn killing of surplus animals for which there will be no food during the coming winter, and the midwinter festival when the day is at its lowest ebb.

There are, in fact, two natural, rural calendars, namely, an agricultural and a pastoral. The agricultural is illustrated by the still extant quarter days — Lady Day

(25 March); Midsummer (24 June); Michaelmas (29 September) and Christmas (25 December). The pastoral is represented by the old Celtic quarter days, which are Imbolc (1 February), Beltane (1 May), Lugnasad (1 August) and Samhain (1 November). Imbolc seems to have been a lambing festival, when the new crop of lambs were born; Beltane marked the date when new grazing could be expected to be ready; Lugnasad probably fixed a date when the shearing was finished and fairs were held to exchange stock; Samhain saw the rounding-up of the flocks and herds, the slaughter of the surplus animals and the mating of the sheep.

The pastoral is the earlier of the two and has largely lost its identity through being submerged by the later agricultural calendar. The old feast-days were, however, taken over and remembered under different names. Imbolc became Candlemas Day; Beltane was May Day; Lugnasad was transposed into Lammas-tide (the festival of the first-fruits); and Samhain became Martinmas, though with a greater emphasis being placed on its eve, which, of course, is Hallowe'en. (Beltane) Candlemas, Whit Sunday, Lammas and Martinmas are still official Scottish Term Days.

The agricultural calendar itself, though it preceded Christianity, was in due course overtaken and Christianised, the mediaeval ecclesiastical calendar being overwhelmed with a plethora of saints' days. Candlemas Day was held to mark the anniversary of the Purification of the Virgin Mary; Easter, though retaining the name of an old Norse goddess, celebrated Christ's resurrection; Hallowe'en, with its long and ineradicable association with the free-roving spirits of the dead, became All Saints' Day; and the very important date of the winter solstice was made the special mass or festival of Christ Himself.

The composite calendar which resulted was complex, its threads needing considerable unravelling before we can understand just why a certain festival was held on a certain date. Nevertheless it served its purpose very well. It enabled the conservative peasantry to keep up their old festivals at the traditional times without offending the priest. And the multiplicity of saints' days seemed a providential arrangement for giving hard-worked country folk an adequate number of holidays, — bearing in mind that holidays were, in their origin, 'holy-days'.

Today, with a five-day working week commonplace, a four-day week looming, and an annual holiday of some weeks taken more or less for granted, the need for numerous breaks disguised as saints' days has passed. A few of the main festivals are retained, though even they are being superseded. Whitsuntide has been eclipsed by the new Spring Bank Holiday, and the transfer of August Bank Holiday to the end of the month has effectually severed the link between it and Lammas-tide. The fires that were once lit on Samhain and were later associated with St Martin have for the past 300 years served to commemorate that unlikely character, Guy Fawkes.

Yet in the countryside vestiges of the old traditions still abound. In Wales, sheep-shearing is still a communal effort, when neighbours go from farm to farm assisting with the work, while their wives gather in the farm kitchen to prepare an evening feast from a slaughtered sheep. The bounds of country parishes are still beaten on Rogationtide. Superstitions are still attached to the use of evergreens at Christmas, most incumbents banning mistletoe from their churches, for instance. And old beliefs connected with the soil and the calendar linger. A grand old countryman of my acquaintance once told me that Good Friday was 'the day hardained by the Lord for plantin' tetties'. And not long ago a gardener informed me that the very best date for planting broad beans was 5 November, Bonfire Night.

Other ancient customs have been revived largely as a result of the revolution in transport enabling commuters and retired folk to live in rural villages, In search of pegs on which to hang social events, they unearth memories of old-time harvest homes and May-day celebrations, and soon Morris dancers are prancing and Harvest Home speeches are being made in places where no-one living had ever seen or heard them. There is hardly a church in the land which does not now have a Harvest Festival, though it was not much more than a hundred years ago that Robert Hawker started the first one in Cornwall. The newly-popular cult of weaving corn-dollies, or kern babies, from straw serves to keep alive almost-forgotten traditions about the primeval Corn Goddess.

The essence of a rural festival is that it serves a useful purpose. Modern revivals of ancient customs qualify in that respect, for most of them are concerned with the very practical aim of raising money. In the village where I was brought up, the Cricket Club had a centenary match whenever it was in urgent need of funds! No records existed of matches played a hundred years earlier, so no-one could contradict the officers when they proclaimed a grand centenary, and everyone rallied to support an event which raised cash for new sports gear and was good fun anyway. I saw recently a report of a Wiltshire village advertising a Bustard Feast. I am convinced that no such celebration existed there when I was a boy, but good luck to the organisers. I am sure their instinct was sound.

Much effort has been expended over the last few decades in collecting memories and scraps of dialogue from old mumming plays. They are rightly hailed as examples of old folk drama. But such recollections as have survived into the twentieth century owe nothing to the literati of past centuries, who in general regarded these effusions of the poor with tolerant contempt. The mumming plays survived for one reason only, and that was that they gave the poor of the parish an opportunity for tapping the inhabitants of the 'big house' for Christmas largesse. In virtually every version of the Christmas Mumming Play is an indigent rascal, usually called Little Johnny Jack, who pleads for alms, on the grounds that he has about 14 children to keep. And sometimes Father Christmas, who normally appears as a compère, adds his request for 'mince-pies, plum pudding, a pot of good Christmas ale' and other good provender from 'the noble company'.

Our ancestors had a sure instinct for holding on to anything that served a practical purpose. We have not entirely lost it.

CHAPTER 2

Twelfth Night and Plough Monday

THE REAL turning-point in the cycle of the year is, of course, the winter solstice, 21 December. From that time onwards the days almost imperceptibly lengthen, even though the worst winter weather normally lies ahead. Men have long been aware of the significance of the winter solstice and have celebrated with a midwinter feast the moment when the sun ceased to flee into the darkness and began its long journey towards spring.

But the manipulation of the calendar in the year 1752 produced some rather awkward anomalies, apart from near-riots by simple folk who thought they were being robbed of 11 days of their lives. The situation arose, of course, through an error in the Julian Calendar, which was adopted by most western European countries from the 6th century A.D. onwards. The equinoctial year does not lend itself to simplification by decimalisation or any other means, for it contains an awkward fraction in that it comprises 365.2422 days. The Julian calendar attempted to deal with that fraction by making every fourth year a leap year, of 366 days. This helped, but the devisers of the Julian calendar were trapped into error by applying the rule to *every* fourth year. They should have excluded the last year of a century, except when that year is divisible by 400. Thus, the year 1600 would be a leap year, but the year 1700 would not.

By the sixteenth century the error amounted to ten days. What should, according to the original calculations, have been 11 March was now 21 March. Accordingly in 1582 Pope Gregory XIII introduced what has ever since been known as the Gregorian Calendar. Ten days were dropped, to eliminate the accumulated error, and from henceforth leap years were dealt with in the proper manner.

Most of the Catholic countries adopted the new style of reckoning in that year of

1582, and most of the rest of Europe followed in 1583. But Protestant England would have nothing to do with it until 1752. By then the error had grown to 11 days, which were accordingly sliced from the calendar between 3 September and 14 September of that year.

The change gave rise to considerable confusion and controversy. Ought the dates of certain traditional events to be calculated according to the old or the new calendar? Wassailing the apple trees, for instance. In the West Country apple orchards were traditionally wassailed on the Eve of Twelfth Night, which was by the old reckoning 4 January. But if the calendar had not been tampered with, Christmas would now be on 5 January, and Twelfth Night would therefore be 17 January. The apples ought therefore to be wassailed on 16 January. Which date was the correct one?

Seeking for a sign, great crowds gathered at Glastonbury at Christmas (new date) 1752, to see what the sacred thorn would do. Local tradition asserted that the thorn was a descendant of one that had sprung from the staff of Joseph of Arimathea when he brought the Christian gospel to Somerset within a few decades of the Crucifixion. It had the reputation of always coming into bloom on Christmas Day, and, indeed, in 1645 a clergyman, Rev. John Eachard, quoted the fact as proof that 25 December was Christ's birthday. So the crowds assembled to see whether the thorn would adapt itself to the new calendar.

It did not. No blossoms appeared till 5 January — the appointed time by the old style of reckoning. Nature and supernature were therefore obviously adhering to the old calendar, and a wise man would follow their example. Hence the proper date for wassailing apple trees in the West Country still remains 16 January — the Eve of Twelfth Night (old style).

The wassailing of the apple trees almost became extinct a few years ago. At one time it was thought that the old custom was followed in only two places in Somerset, at one of which it was discontinued in 1976. That report was over pessimistic, for I know of four or five places in the West Country where wassailing is carried out in some years at least, though perhaps not regularly. The one which now receives most publicity is the ceremony performed on a convenient date in mid-January at Monty's Court, Norton Fitzwarren, near Taunton, the home of Colonel C. T. Mitford-Slade, the lord lieutenant of Somerset. It owes its continuance to adoption by the Taunton Cider Company.

'Wassail' comes from a couple of old Saxon words meaning 'good health'. Good health to both the apple trees and the cider drinkers. The party at Norton Fitzwarren generally numbers several hundreds of cider devotees, who assemble in a large marquee and drink mulled cider, or Wassail Punch, piping hot. Thus fortified, they venture out into the orchard, where the frost is being dispelled by a leaping bonfire. A group of burly Somerset lads hoist the Wassail Queen upon their shoulders. Her duty is to lodge an offering of toast soaked in cider in a fork of each of the apple trees and to pour a libation of cider around the trunk. Behind her marches a firing-squad of farmers with muzzle-loading guns, with which they discharge volleys through the branches. Musicians with a collection of antique

1 Wassailing Apple Trees at Carhampton, Somerset, 1936. Guns are fired into the tree branches while the Wassailing Song is sung

brass instruments, led by an accordion, strike up the Wassailing Song, in which everybody joins. Then three lusty cheers before moving on to the next tree. The version of the Wassailing Song Sung at Norton Fitzwarren runs:

> *Old Apple-tree, Old Apple-tree,*
> *We wassail thee, and hoping thou wilt bear,*
> *For the Lord doth know where we shall be*
> *Till apples come another year;*
> *For to bear well, and to bloom well,*
> *So merry let us be;*
> *Let every man take off his hat and shout to thee,*
> *Old Apple Tree, Old Apple Tree;*
> *We wassail thee and hoping thou wilt bear*
> *Hat fulls,*
> *Cap fulls,*
> *And three bushel bag fulls,*
> *And a little heap under the stairs.*

There are many other versions, some with many verses, but most of them bring in the reference to 'the little heap under the stairs' — a nice, homely touch, nostalgic for anyone who has been brought up in apple country.

Wassailing naturally flourished chiefly in the orchards of western England. It was once common in all counties from Devon to Herefordshire, and there are references to it in Yorkshire and Nottinghamshire, but I have never heard of it in East Anglia and the adjacent counties.

The wassailing ceremony at Norton Fitzwarren is a much more light-hearted affair than it used to be. In its origin it was essentially a family occasion. The procession was headed and the offerings of toast and cider were presented not by a Wassail Queen but by a grandfather, the oldest member of the clan. All the family had to be there, or ill-luck would follow. Although there was an element of merry-making, the ceremony was carried out with some reverence and, indeed, took on something of the nature of a sacrament. It established an identity of interest between the apple trees and the family, which was, to some extent, dependent on them. The cider-soaked toast and the cider were token acknowledgments of what the trees had provided during the past year. The homage and the song were encouragement to them to repeat the performance in the year ahead.

Some of the details may repay closer investigation. Countrymen have told folklorists that the soaked toast was wedged into the branches specifically 'for the robins', and both the robin and the wren have been considered sacred birds in ancient mythology. So too was the blue tit, and in a Devonshire version, written down in 1876, 'a little boy was hoisted up into the tree and seated on a branch. He was to represent a tom-tit and was to sit there crying, "Tit, tit, more to eat"; upon which some of the bread and cheese and cider was handed up to him.' The song which concluded this Devonshire ceremony was almost exactly the same as the Somerset one quoted above.

The popular current explanation of the firing of a volley into the branches of the tree is that it drives away evil spirits. I think it is more likely, however, intended to waken the god or goddess of the apple tree from the midwinter slumber. It is probably on a par with the Biblical story of Elijah urging the prophets of Baal to 'shout louder; perhaps he is asleep and needs to be awakened'. Some versions of wassailing customs, dating from before the widespread use of firearms, say that the boles of the trees were beaten with sticks, the threshing being accompanied by as much noise as could be made by banging tin trays and kettles with pokers.

In a collection of information on *The Origin and Meaning of Apple Cults* (1919) J. Rendel Harris quotes a West Sussex instance illustrating the importance attached to every member of the family being present.

'Last New Year's Eve the mother of a sick boy told me that her poor child was sadly put out because he was not able to worsle his grandfather's apple trees. And it is quite certain that both mother and child expected a total failure of the apple crop in the grandfather's orchard to follow the omission.'

In West Sussex, however, the wassailing seems to have been usually performed by a party of local wassailers who went round to the various orchards in turn. In the account given by Mr Harris, 'Farmers give a few pence to the worslers, who form a circle round the trees and sing at the top of their voices:

> *Stand fast root;*
> *Bear well top;*
> *Pray God send us*
> *A good howling crop.*
>> *Every twig,*
>> *Apples big,*
>> *Every bough,*
>> *Apples enow.*
> *Hats full; caps full,*
> *Full quarter sacks full,*
> *Holla, boys, holla! Huzza!*

and then all shout in chorus, with the exception of one boy, who blows a loud blast on a cow's horn.'

Jacqueline Simpson, in *The Folklore of Sussex* (1973), provides the additional information that at Duncton, in West Sussex, wassailing was carried on along these lines until the 1920s. The wassailers were organised by a 'Captain of the Wassailers', one Spratty Knight. Starting from the inn, they went to each farm in turn and asked, 'Do you want your trees wassailed?'

The performance was much as described above, for Somerset. Then 'everyone trooped out of the orchard up to the farmhouse door, where they were greeted by the farmer's wife with drinks and goodies. Sometimes money was given instead of good cheer.'

This seems to mark a transitional stage between the essentially family wassailing and what some folklorists call 'The Visiting Wassail'. In the Visiting Wassail a party of wassailers go round to houses in the neighbourhood, singing the wassailing song, drinking to the health of the occupants, and inviting refreshment. It apparently has no necessary connection with apple trees and can occur at any convenient date over the Christmas season.

The songs sung by the Visiting Wassailers show much more variation than do those devoted to invoking the apple tree spirit, and yet there are often striking similarities. In *The Folklore of the Cotswolds* Katharine M. Briggs gives the following version from Minchinhampton, Gloucestershire:

> *Wassail, wassail all over the town,*
> *Our bread is white, our ale it is brown;*
> *Our bowl is made of the mapling tree,*
> *To my wassailing bowl I drink unto thee.*
> *Here's health to our master and to his right eye.*
> *God send our master a good Christmas pie!*

A good Christmas pie that we may all see,
To my wassailing bowl I drink unto thee . . . .

Other verses wish the master 'a barrel of good beer, a good crop of corn, and a jolly fat pig'.

Compare the similarities and the differences in the following verse from the Langport (Somerset) Wassailing Song:

Wassail, wassail all over the town;
Your cup it is white, and your beer it is brown;
Your bowl it is made of the good ashen tree;
And your beer it is brewed of the best barley;
Langport bull-dog have lost his big tail
In the night that we go, a-singing wassail.

The chorus is:

The Black Dog of Langport have a-burned off his tail;
And this is the night of our jolly wassail;
  Vor tis our wassail,
  And tis your wassail,
And joy be to you, vor tis our wassail.

Local antiquarians have linked the Black Dog of Langport with the Danes, who were defeated by King Alfred in the neighbourhood in the year 878. If so, it is a remarkable example of folk memory bridging the centuries.

Wendy Boase, in *The Folklore of Hampshire* (1976), quotes a very similar verse recorded at Yarmouth, in the Isle of Wight. There it is the cup which is white, and the bowl is made of the 'ashen tree', as in Somerset. J. Rendel Harris also gives a Devon version in which, again, it is the cup that is white but in which the bowl is of maplewood.

He also quotes a very different song which was recorded for Devon but which I have heard in Somerset. It sounds more like a full-blooded drinking song, but I am assured that it was used in wassailing:

There was an old man,
And he had an old cow,
And how to keep her he didn't know how;
  So he built her a barn
  To keep this cow warm,
And a little more cider would do us no harm.
  Harm, my boys, harm!
  Harm, my boys, harm!
And a little more cider would do us no harm.

Some of the older collections of folklore suggest a more elaborate wassailing ceremony. In *The Folklore of the Cotswolds* (1974) Katharine M. Briggs quotes from the magazine, *Folklore*, 1912:

'Wassailers still go round at Randwick, Woodchester, Avening, Minchinhampton, the outskirts of Stroud and probably many other villages. They
formerly had a large wooden (maple) bowl, which at Minchinhampton was kept
during the year in the possession of one man known as "King of the
Wassailers". It was decorated with evergreens and small dolls. The latter are
now omitted, and a modern bowl is used, with quite a bower of greenery and
coloured paper over-arching it. Money is dropped into the bowl, and spent on
drink. An old woman of 78 can remember when there were as many as twenty
of these wassailers in Minchinhampton; now there are but three or four.'

Note that the drink here is beer, not cider, and that there is no mention of
apple trees. Summarising information about wassailing collected in 1902, the
editor of *Folklore* commented:

'The favourite liquor was "lamb's-wool", — a mixture of ale, spices and
roasted apples. In many places parties of wassailers went about visiting the
neighbouring houses, singing their good wishes and carrying a bowl with
apples, which the hosts were expected to fill with ale, or money to purchase it.'

The Gentleman's Magazine for 1794 records an interesting appendix to the
ceremony of wassailing the apple trees in South Devon. After the wassailing is
completed, by the men of the family only,

'They return to the house, the doors of which they are sure to find bolted by the
females, who, be the weather what it may, are inexorable to all entreaties to
open them till someone has guessed at what is on the spit, which is generally
some nice little thing, difficult to be hit on, and is the reward of him who first
names it. The doors are then thrown open, and the lucky clodpole receives the
titbit as his recompense. Some are so superstitious as to believe that if they
neglect this custom the trees will bear no apples that year.'

Finally, John Brand, in his *Observations on Popular Antiquities* (1900), gives a
decidedly different approach to the subject of wassailing. He says that on the
evening of Twelfth Day, in Herefordshire

'The farmers with their friends and servants meet together, and about six
o'clock walk out to a field where wheat is growing. In the highest part of the
ground twelve small fires and one large one are lighted up. The attendants,
headed by the master of the family, pledge the company in old cider, which
circulates freely . . . . A circle is formed around the large fire, when a general
shout and hallooing takes place, which you hear answered from all the adjacent
villages and fields. Sometimes fifty or sixty of these fires may all be seen at once.
    'This being finished, the company returns home, where the good housewife
and her maids are preparing a good supper. A large cake is always provided,
with a hole in the middle. After supper the company will attend the bailiff (or
head of the oxen) to the wain-house, where the following particulars are
observed. The master, at the head of his friends, fills the cup (generally of the

strongest ale) and stands opposite the first or finest of the oxen. He then pledges him with a curious toast; the company follow his example with all the other oxen, addressing each by his name. This being finished, the large cake is produced and with much ceremony put on the horn of the first ox, through the hole above mentioned. The ox is then tickled, to make him toss his head. If he throws the cake behind, then it is the mistress's perquisite; if before, the bailiff himself claims the prize. The company then return to the house, the doors of which they find locked, nor will they be opened till some joyous songs are sung.'

Here again we have the curious custom, origin unknown, of locking out the participants in the wassailing ceremony until they have performed a feat — in this instance, merely singing some songs.

The Gloucestershire custom of carrying round a bowl when wassailing was also observed in Sussex. Jacqueline Simpson, in *The Folklore of Sussex* (1973), records the evidence of a member of Shipley Women's Institute who remembered that when she was a child, 'the children would go round the village with gaily decorated baskets or china bowls covered with a cloth; in return for a penny or a cake, they would lift the cloth and let the giver have a peep at their "wassail bowl" . . . .'

Perhaps in the original version there were two dolls, representing the Virgin and Child, in the bowl.

Miss Simpson also mentions that in Sussex

'Many wassail parties were held on New Year's Eve, and as the evening began to approach the hour of twelve, a large china bowl filled with hot spiced ale was brought in and placed in the centre of a round table in the middle of the room. On top of the ale floated "lamb's wool" — the white fluffy inside of roasted apples, which looked like lamb's wool. Everyone present was given a silver spoon, and, forming themselves into a procession, they walked around the table (clockwise), singing and stirring the ale at the same time. When the clock struck twelve, glasses were filled from the bowl, and everyone wished each other "good wassail".'

The Cornish wassail customs seem to be an amalgam of most of those pertaining to other counties. In *The Folklore of Cornwall* (1975) Tony Deane and Tony Shaw record that in Bodmin the wassail bowl was carried from door to door by four men in evening dress. They collected for charity and sang a short wassail song. This was done on Christmas Eve, not on the Eve of Twelfth Night, though in other parts of Cornwall wassailing continued throughout the Christmas period, until New Year's Eve.

'The Truro Wassailers', say the authors, 'with their gaily-decorated apple-wood bowl, form a tightly-knit community, each family preserving the right to carry on the Wassail until the last member has died, then passing on the honour to another family. They sing outside houses and inns, beginning with this verse:

Now Christmas is over, our Wassail begins,
Pray open the door and let us come in,

and beg for money or drink without embarrassment:

Now we poor Wassail Boys are growing weary and cold,
Drop a small piece of silver into our Bowl,

then deliver their blessing:

I hope that your apple-trees will prosper and bear,
And bring forth good cider when we come next year.'

The account is given in the present tense, and the authors state that the custom is still being continued.

We are back to cider again, and so, lamb's wool and ale notwithstanding, let me supply a recipe for Wassail Punch, with cider as its main ingredient:

Wassail Punch (quantities given should be enough for 10 or 12 persons).

5 quarts of a dry cider;	¼-teaspoonful grated nutmeg;
7 tablespoonfuls of brown sugar;	2 bananas;
3 sliced oranges;	¼-teaspoonful grated cinnamon.
4 cloves;	

Heat the cider slowly with the sugar, sliced oranges and spices until it is almost boiling. Pour into a bowl, add the bananas, thinly sliced, and serve at once.

Just the thing to keep out the cold, let alone evil spirits, on a frosty January night.

*   *   *

Is it really true that our peasant ancestors had twelve days of holiday at Christmas? It depends, of course, on what one means by holiday. On a farm there are chores that have to be done, come Sunday, Bank Holiday, Christmas or any other festival. The domestic animals have to be fed and given fresh litter to lie on; the cows have to be milked; calving cows have to be attended to; water drawn from the well; the woodpile replenished. Indoors any housewife will testify that there is no respite from cleaning, preparing meals, washing up and attending to the needs of the children. What else, in the middle of winter, was there for the peasant to do? The answer is, work in the fields — ploughing, hauling and spreading farmyard manure, hedging and ditching. These were the tasks that were abandoned during the Twelve Days of Christmas. Until well into the nineteenth century horses were blooded in mid-winter. Their owners thought that their blood became too rich and overheated through spending so much time idle in the stables, so they released some of it by making an incision in the jugular vein. The traditional date for the operation was St Stephen's Day, 26 December, doubtless because the horses then had ten days or so to recover before they were required to do any more work.

Wassailing was one of many activities with which villagers filled the festival days (and nights). Most of them fell into disuse centuries ago and have been lost in the mists of time, but traces may still be discovered by those who search. Most cluster around Twelfth Night, the climax of the festivities. Cornwall has a tradition of 'guizing' or 'geese-dancing'. The word is derived from 'disguise' and refers to the practice of the dancers disguising themselves by fantastic costumes and headgear. Apparently they used to perform plays which were very similar to the mumming plays common to much of England. Christina Hole *(English Custom & Usage,* 1941) says that one of the regular dancers in the Land's End district used to wear a bullock's head. Also that up to 1892 among the dancers at Wainfleet in Lincolnshire was one who was dressed in skins with a wisp of straw in his mouth, to represent a pig. Most Dorset villages used to have an 'Ooser' — a terrifying creature in a bull mask, who used to appear in sundry revels during the Christmas holiday. One survived at Melbury Osmond until the beginning of the present century.

The revelry on Twelfth Night used at one time to be so uninhibited and exuberant that it was thought necessary to appoint a 'King of Misrule', to give events some semblance of respectability. On Exmoor it is remembered that the 'King' was elected by the device of baking a plum-cake with a bean in it and distributing the slices. He who got the slice with the bean was King for the day. By Victorian times the custom had been decorously transformed into a parlour event; the cake contained both a bean and a pea, the girl who found the pea becoming Queen of the family party. R. W. Patten *(Exmoor Custom and Song,* 1974) records that a wassail bean dance, evidently a revival, took place at Holford as late as 1930:

'As alcohol was not allowed in the village hall, a bowl was filled with beans, some bearing numbers. Each dancer was invited to draw a bean from the bowl. When the music stopped a number was drawn from a hat, and the possessor of the bean bearing the corresponding number received a prize of five shillings.'

Another long-obsolete custom was the wassailing of the bees. The only reference I have found to it is in Jacqueline Simpson's *The Folklore of Sussex* (1973), where it is noted that beehives were being wassailed in Sussex around 1827. A little later the then vicar of Amberley recorded the words of a song sung to the bees on Twelfth Night, as remembered by an old man in his parish:

> *Bees, oh bees of Paradise,*
> *Does the work of Jesus Christ,*
> *Does the work which no man can.*
> *God made bees, and bees made honey;*
> *God made man, and man made money.*
> *God made great men to plough and to sow,*
> *And God made little boys to tend the rooks and crows;*
> *God made women to brew and to bake,*

And God made little girls to eat up all the cake.
Then blow the horn!

As a boy in Wiltshire I was familiar with the middle lines of this verse but never heard of it being used in the context of beehive wassailing.

A Scottish custom anchored in the Twelve Days of Christmas was Handsel Monday, traditionally the first Monday of the New Year. A handsel is the equivalent of a Christmas box, and this was the day when the servants and tradesmen received their Christmas gifts. In the Scottish countryside the custom was attached to Auld Handsel Monday — the first Monday after 12 January — doubtless through loyalty to the old Julian calendar. *Chambers' Book of Days* (1864) records that

> 'farmers used to treat the whole of their servants on that morning to a liberal breakfast of roast and boiled, with ale, whiskey and cake, to their utmost contentment; after which the guests went about seeing their friends for the remainder of the day. It was also the day on which any disposed for change gave up their places, and when new servants were engaged.'

Chambers' Book of Days also describes a custom observed at Pauntley, in Gloucestershire, on the Twelfth Day:

> 'All the servants of every farmer assemble in one of the fields that has been sown with wheat. At the end of twelve lands they make twelve fires in a row with straw; around one of which, larger than the rest, they drink a cheerful glass of cider to their master's health, and success to the future harvest; then, returning home, they feast on cakes made with carraways, soaked in cider, which they claim as a reward for their past labour in sowing the grain.'

Strangely, this was held to be effective as a prevention of smut in the wheat crop. (A 'land', incidentally, is one of the sections into which a field is normally divided by ploughing; also known as a 'rudge'.)

The one Twelfth Night custom which is still widely remembered is that of taking down the Christmas decorations. Many housewives consider it unlucky not to do so. It is, in fact, a dramatic recognition that the holiday is over and that normal work is about to be resumed.

The Monday after Twelfth Night is traditionally Plough Monday — a day associated with many rural customs. The fullest account I have found of them refers to Cambridgeshire and is in Enid Porter's *Cambridgeshire Customs and Folklore* (1969). Nearly every example refers to the past, most of the customs surviving not later than about the end of the nineteenth century, though a notice dated 1937 is quoted to the effect that 'in Toft the day would be the occasion that year for the men of the village to go over to Kingston for a supper of salt beef, carrots and potatoes at the Chequers. This was to be followed by a concert of old songs sung to the accompaniment of a pianist from Cambridge.'

In Swaffham Prior schoolboys with blackened faces used to carry round a miniature plough to the bigger houses, where they would sing a verse and ask for money. This went on until about 1929. Earlier the custom was for men to drag a plough through the villages, asking for alms and threatening to plough up the doorstep of any householder refusing. The money collected was later used for beer, during an evening of dancing and revelry. At Brandon Creek, however, some of the cash was spent on groceries, which were stuffed into women's drawers, tied at the bottom, and given to needy old women.

In many villages the dancers were dressed in fantastic costumes, and in many instances they had their faces blackened, — a token disguise. The dance was a version of the Morris dance, and some of the characters depicted were identical with those in mumming plays. The Cambridge Folk Museum has a copy of a song, dated 1861, which was sung by the 'Madingley Plough Boys'. From allusions in it to the Queen and the Prince of Wales it looks as though it was composed not long before that date.

By the end of the century, says Enid Porter, the old custom 'had degenerated into a somewhat rough affair with little organised dancing. Many elderly Cambridge residents can recall being frightened, as children, by noisy groups of black-faced men and youths, often intoxicated, going about the streets demanding money'. So the celebrations fell into disrepute and, frowned on by respectable folk, died a natural death.

In earlier times, however, the Plough Monday customs were widely observed. Christina Hole (*English Custom and Usage,* 1941) gives examples from Lincolnshire, Yorkshire, Leicestershire, Nottinghamshire and Northumberland, as well as Cambridgeshire. Enid Porter (*The Folklore of East Anglia,* 1974) states that Plough Monday used to be celebrated in most East Anglian villages. Jacqueline Simpson, researching for *The Folklore of Sussex* (1973), could find only one vague reference to Plough Monday celebrations in that county. Place and date were unrecorded, but all the essentials were there — 'dressed all in white', 'garlands of paper flowers hung round their necks, and bits of ribbon pinned all over, an' they dragged a plough round an' asked for money at every house'. Afterwards 'they had a festival, an' the prettiest girl in the village was always chosen to sit at the head of the table. She was always called Bessie.' Significantly, Enid Porter records the name 'Bessie' in Cambridgeshire. There he was the last man in the procession, who used to collect the alms in a wooden spoon. And usually he was dressed as a woman. The same evidence is offered in *Chambers' Book of Days* (1864) by an eyewitness of Plough Monday celebrations in Lincolnshire. Here too Bessie was the man who carried the money-box. He 'formerly wore a bullock's tail behind, under his gown, and which he held in his hand while dancing'. This observer mentions that most of the classes of farm worker attended, each wearing the badge of his trade. Thus threshers carried flails, carters cracked their whips; even smiths and millers were represented.

In the Cleveland district of Yorkshire the Plough Monday festivities were associated with sword-dancing. The sword-dancing team was known as Plough Stots. In the 1930s the late Rolf Gardiner, of Fontmell Magna, near Shaftesbury, took the Plough Stots as the pattern for a revival of sword-dancing on Plough Monday which he organised in Dorset and the neighbouring counties. In 1938 he took his sword-dancers in an old estate lorry on a tour of Dorset towns. They performed their dance in Blandford, Dorchester, Cerne Abbas, Sherborne, Stalbridge, Sturminster Newton and Shaftesbury, all in one day. Later they went into Wiltshire, Berkshire and Oxfordshire.

An account of the dance, which puts the event in its proper context and explains the thinking which prompted it, was given in the *Western Gazette* on 14 January 1938:

'In the Plough Dance — which was witnessed by the Minister of Agriculture — not only was a traditional custom resuscitated, but the idea of the consecration of the plough and of the earnest collaboration between men and the forces of the earth was symbolised in dramatic form. The Fool, representing the spirit of the year, after providing amusement for the onlookers, is killed by the sword-dancers, who perform a mock funeral procession around him as he lies dead on the ground. The ceremonial plough now moves around the dancers in a circle and penetrates their ranks; where, at its fertilizing touch and the cry of "Speed the Plough", the Fool springs to life; and the dancers finally move off, dragging the plough behind them. The Springhead Sword-dancers had no intention of merely reviving an ancient custom. They wished by the gaiety, humour and power of the dance and its dramatic representation of the death and resurrection of the year, to recall to all who saw them the meaning of Plough Monday, the day after the Christmas season, when men remember that, without the cultivation of the soil and the existence of skilled countrymen, civilized life on the Earth could not endure.'

That is a truth which needs increasing emphasis in this sophisticated urban age. It is a pity that so soon after the valiant attempt by the Springhead Sword-dancers their initiative was extinguished by the advent of war.

However, the religious connotations of the plough celebrations are not entirely forgotten. Kingsley Palmer *(The Folklore of Somerset,* 1976) says that at Hambridge, in Somerset, the first Sunday after Twelfth Night 'was and still is known as Plough Sunday. The plough is brought into the church and blessed, and this is looked upon as an important contribution to successful ploughing in preparation for spring sowing.'

I think there may be other examples of the revival of this laudable old custom.

Happy countrymen, who could regard the resumption of work after a holiday as an occasion for rejoicing! For them the growing of food as well as the eating of it was a normal part of life. Work and play were inextricably mingled, and all was sanctified by association with the still mysterious power which, in response to man's labours in the fields, produces life and growth.

In some districts the Kern Baby, or Corn Dolly, which had been fashioned from the last stalks of corn cut at the previous harvest and which had had a place of honour by the hearth all through the autumn, was taken out on Plough Monday

2 Corn Dolly,
representing the Corn
Goddess, from Whalton,
Northumberland.
Making corn dollies is an
ancient craft recently
revived

and reverently laid in the first furrow. It held, so it was thought, the spirit of the
Corn Goddess, who gave life to the sown seed. The plough turned over the soil in
a brown, curving wave to bury her, and there she was, safe in the womb of the
earth, ready to accomplish her annual miracle. From death came life; from
darkness, light; it was always so in the cycle of the country year.

*   *   *

A few other customs pertaining to the end of the twelve days of holiday and the resumption of work remain to be noticed.

An alternative name for Plough Monday, though not apparently so widely used, was St Distaff's Day. Not that there ever was a St Distaff. The name was merely a reminder that on that day the distaff side of the family was expected to start work, too. As Robert Herrick puts it in his *Hesperides* (1648):

> *Partly worke and partly play,*
> *You must on St Distaff's Day;*
> *From the plough soon free your teame;*
> *Then come home and fother them;*
> *If the Maides a-spinning goe,*
> *Burne the flax and fire the tow,*
> *Scorch the plackets, but beware*
> *That ye singe no maiden-haire.*
> *Bring in pailes of water then,*
> *Let the maides bewash the men.*
> *Give St. Distaff all the right;*
> *then bid Christmas-sport good-night.*
> *And next morrow, everyone*
> *To his owne vocation.*

Some of the references to an obsolete craft mean little to us, but the general idea is clear. The transition from holiday to work-day was gradual. The ploughmen stopped work early and came home for a last fling, the 'maides' participating, before settling down to the winter routine on the day *after* Plough Monday.

Something similar is hinted at in the East Anglian customs associated with the day after Plough Monday. In Whittlesey, Cambridgeshire, it was known as Straw Bear Tuesday. Enid Porter, in *Cambridgeshire Customs and Folklore* (1969), quotes a letter dated 1909 in which the writer states:

'When I was at Whittlesey yesterday I had the pleasure of meeting a straw bear . . . . I had not been at Whittlesey on the day for 40 years and feared the custom had died out. In my boyhood the straw bear was a man completely swathed in straw, led by a string by another, and made to dance in front of people's houses, in return for which money was expected. This always took place on the Tuesday following Plough Monday. Yesterday the straw bear was a boy, and there was no dancing. Otherwise there was no change.'

Other observations quoted by Enid Porter indicate that the Bear was 'one of the confraternity of the Plough', who dressed up and engaged in a clumsy dance to entertain 'the good folk who had on the previous day subscribed to the rustics' spread of beer, tobacco and beef, at which the Bear had presided'. His appearance was thus a thank-you gesture. Why the animal chosen should be a bear is not known. But evidently he was made an excuse for extending the long Christmas festivities for just one more day.

CHAPTER 3

The Lean Days

I T IS NOT easy for us to imagine life without shops, and particularly without food shops. We are so used to filling our baskets from the well-stocked shelves of supermarkets, which draw their supplies from half the countries in the world, that to have to depend on the produce of our own gardens and the adjacent fields is almost inconceivable. Yet, with infrequent exceptions, that has been the lot of the majority of the human race since before the beginning of history.

Not long ago I had to prepare, for comparison, typical diet sheets for average families in the United Kingdom, India and West Africa. While the Indian and West African families were still relying on locally-produced foods, I found that the British family was drawing supplies from at least ten countries, for a simple menu for one day. As a matter of interest, the countries were the U.S.A. (cornflakes and baked beans), Jamaica (sugar), India (tea), Canada (flour for bread), Holland (butter), Denmark (bacon), Israel (oranges for marmalade), Kenya (coffee), New Zealand (meat), Nigeria (cocoa); and the eggs, milk and vegetables probably came from counties scores of miles away.

Yet I myself can remember when, in the village household where I was reared, the number of countries represented on our table would have been reduced to three — Jamaica, India and Nigeria. We baked bread from wheat from our own fields, drank milk from our cows, ate butter made from that milk, killed our own pigs for bacon and our sheep for meat (though rabbits were a more frequent meat dish), and collected eggs from the farmyard hens. We knew nothing of cornflakes and baked beans, and oranges appeared only at Christmas. We had home-made jam instead of marmalade.

This was in the 1920s, when basic supplies could be bought at a tiny shop in the village. A generation or so earlier lacked even that amenity. The 1851 census (the first which gives details of households and their occupations) reveals no shop in our village. No doubt the carrier brought home some food on his return from his weekly visits to the market town, six miles away. In an earlier book, *A Family and a Village,* I describe how an old market woman used to trudge over the hills to the town, carrying a heavy basket of eggs, butter and poultry and return with an equally burdensome load of meat cuttings or fish to sell at cottages en route. But often in winter even these tenuous links would be cut by snowdrifts for weeks at a time, and the village would fall back on its own resources.

Not many centuries earlier the entire country had to rely, for the most part, on a similar self-sufficiency. In his book *The Darien Disaster* John Prebble describes the preparations in Scotland for planting a colony on the Isthmus of Darien, in Central America, in 1698. The fleet that assembled at Edinburgh that July consisted of only five ships, the largest of 350 tons, and the prospective colonists numbered about 1200 men. Yet to provision this meagre armada stretched Scotland's resources to the limit:

> 'For every ton of meal or cask of beef taken aboard the fleet there were dry fields and empty byres that promised little in replacement . . . . Scotland had stripped its larder and was left with nothing to supply the Colony when needed, and little to help itself through the certainty of a more bitter famine next year.'

Famine. How often the word occurs in mediaeval records. Between 1310 and 1348, when the Black Death struck, no fewer than 15 years are designated 'years of famine'. Famine and pestilence walked together.

It is against this background of self-sufficiency and the disastrous consequences of a harvest failure or an epidemic among livestock that country calendar customs are set. Real hunger was never very far away. A good harvest was an occasion for rejoicing and gratitude. To enter winter with barely adequate provisions aroused fears for one's very survival till the sun shone warm again.

The Twelve Days of Christmas were a season of euphoria. 'Eat, drink and be merry, for tomorrow we die', could well have been the motto of many of the revellers. When at last the festive season could be extended no longer, even by making a festival of the renewal of ploughing, the shortage of provisions began to bite. April, as every countryman knows, is the leanest month of the year, but February and March are austere enough. The ecclesiastical injunction to fast during Lent merely made a virtue out of what was usually a necessity.

The customs and folklore of the countryside during the lean days are therefore loaded with anxiety about the weather and with eager searching for the first signs of spring.

*   *   *

The first calendar landmark of the period is St Paul's Day, 25 January. For some reason, the weather on this date was supposed to forecast the weather for the whole year. And not only the weather; it was a kind of Old Moore's Almanac, offering clues to coming disasters, both natural and man-made. *The Shepherd's Almanack* (1676) summarises the popular beliefs: 'If the sun shines it betokens a good year; if it rain or snow, indifferent; if misty, it predicts a great dearth; if it thunder, great wind, and death of people that year'; while John Gay *(Trivia,* 1716) adds:

> *But if the threatening winds in tempest roar,*
> *Then War shall bathe her wasteful sword in gore.*

The day and its significance are not now remembered in most country districts, but Margaret Killip, in *The Folklore of the Isle of Man* (1975), quotes a Manx saying:

> *St Paul's Day stormy and windy,*
> *Famine in the world and great death of mankind;*
> *Paul's Day fair and clear,*
> *Plenty of corn and meal in the world.*

In *The Folklore of Sussex* (1973) Jacqueline Simpson says that in that county St Hilary's Day, 13 January, was held to be the coldest in the year, but I have not heard of this belief elsewhere.

*   *   *

2 February, Candlemas Day, was regarded as of considerable importance in the country year. Ecclesiastically, it is dedicated to the Purification of the Virgin Mary, but it obviously inherited many of the old beliefs and customs attached to the Celtic Imbolc (1 February) and to associated festivals in the Roman world. Imbolc was a lambing festival, and even now the first week of February is the time when many farms arrange to begin lambing. Although still the depth of winter and requiring special provisions to be made for the shelter of ewes and lambs, the early date offers two great advantages. One is that the lambs are just the right age to make best use of the spring grass when it becomes available; the other, that the lambs are well-grown and ready to catch the lucrative market for them in June and July.

Candlemas, of course, was so-called from the custom of requiring a mother to carry candles on her first visit to the church after childbirth. Though still observed in the Roman Catholic church it was banned by the Church of England in the reign of Edward VI. In its rural context, Candlemas Day was held to mark a milestone in the return of the sun. Katharine Briggs, in *The Folklore of the Cotswolds* (1974), says that candles were lighted to strengthen the power of the sun, but adds that the date also marked the time when certain lights were extinguished. She quotes a writer in the *Annual Record of the Oxfordshire and District Folklore Society* for 1950 as stating: 'On Candlemas Day we always used to have tea without a light, as the days were supposed to have lengthened sufficiently by then to make this possible.'

This was true also in Wiltshire, though the association in my home was not so much with Candlemas but with the first week of February, in which my birthday happens to fall!

The increasing daylight led country folk to look for the first signs of spring. Candlemas Day is said in some districts to be the date when the first snowdrops appear, though probably the association is with the purity which the snowdrops represent, for the flowers may open at any time between mid-January to mid-March. Much of the Candlemas rural lore is admonitory:

> *In the barn on Candlemas Day*
> *Should be half the straw and half the hay.*

The Isle of Man version is:

> *Mary's feast day of the candle;*
> *Half fodder and half fire.*

In other words, on Candlemas Day, in spite of signs of the approach of spring, winter should be reckoned as no more than half over. Half the winter livestock rations and half the household's supply of fuel should be still untouched.

> *As the day lengthens,*
> *So the cold strengthens,*

is still a well-known country proverb, applicable to January and early February.

As on the days of St Paul and St Swithin, the weather on Candlemas Day was held to presage climatic events to come. A Scottish rhyme puts it:

> *If Candlemas Day be dry and fair,*
> *Half the winter's to come, and mair;*
> *If Candlemas Day be wet and foul,*
> *The half of winter's gone to Yule.*

In the Isle of Man, where 2 February is also St Bridget's Day, 'if it was a bright sunny day, there would be snow before May Day, but a wet morning foretold a fine spring' (Margaret Killip in *The Folklore of the Isle of Man*).

Perhaps the matter can be summed up in the cautionary and popular country adage, 'A late spring never deceives'.

In the West Country, where spring generally comes early, Candlemas Day was reckoned to be the best day for sowing beans and peas, though they had to be sown when the moon was waning. A Somerset proverb asserts:

> *On Candlemas Day if the thorn hangs a drop*
> *Then you're sure of a good pea crop.*

Again, the association of a wet Candlemas Day with future good weather and abundance. Katharine Briggs *(The Folklore of the Cotswolds,* 1974) also records the association of Candlemas Day with bean-sowing:

Candlemas Day, put beans in the clay;
Put candles and candlesticks all away.

In some districts the Candlemas Day customs overlapped to St Blaize's Day, 3 February — understandably in Cornwall, where St Blaize is the patron saint of the little town of St Blazey. The old Cornish game of hurling was traditionally played in Candlemas Week, and the custom is still preserved in St Ives and St Columb (though in the latter place on Shrove Tuesday).

*   *   *

St Valentine's Day, 14 February, had only a minor significance in rural folklore. The custom of sending anonymous greeting cards, though an ancient one, has experienced ebbs and flows of popularity. It was at high tide in the sentimental mid-Victorian era and is so again at present, but it is a sophisticated practice, rooted in social life, largely urban. It is, in fact, directly developed from the Roman feasts of Lupercalia, one of the features of which was the choosing of partners for the coming year by drawing lots. The scandalised early Christian bishops tried to suppress the ancient custom, but it died hard. At some time in its subsequent career it seems that the commitment for a year, or even a shorter period, could be compounded for by a gift, if either party was unwilling, and by Victorian times it had become little more than a party charade.

Yet country lore, based on observation, still insisted that mid-February was the time when birds chose their mates, and the analogy was still held to be valid in human experience. So most of the Valentine traditions that survive or are remembered are concerned with methods, usually employed by girls, of discovering a lover. The practice of regarding as one's Valentine the first person of the opposite sex that one sees on the morning of 14 February is still widely observed. In some districts girls would put bay leaves under their pillows on Valentine's Eve, hoping to dream of their future husbands; in others, they wore their stockings inside out.

In certain regions, notably East Anglia, children were accustomed to use the feast-day as an excuse for yet another of their expeditions to their neighbours' houses, singing little rhymes and demanding payment in sweets, cakes or cash. Several of these verses are recorded by Enid Porter in *The Folklore of East Anglia* (1974), but they seem to have little connection with lovers. One with more conventional sentiments, which we also knew in Wiltshire, runs:

Roses are red, violets are blue;
Pinks are sweet and so are you.
If you will be mine I will be thine,
So, good morning, Valentine.

But,

Good morrow, Valentine,
Change yar luck an' I'll change mine.

We are raggety, you are fine,
So pray gon us a Valentine

is straightforward cadging.

R.W. Patten, in *Exmoor Song and Custom* (1974), gives a happy little couplet which neatly expresses the sentiments of the festival:

This is the day birds choose their mate,
And I choose you, if I'm not too late

Miss Porter *(Cambridgeshire Customs & Folklore,* 1969) records that in the Fens north of Ely marshmen prepared their traps for a run of eels during that week; and Christina Hole *(English Custom and Usage,* 1941) states that at Norham-on-Tweed the salmon fishermen and their nets are blessed on 14 February, on which day the season for salmon netting begins.

*   *   *

Almost all the other festivals of the lean days in the cold early months of the year are linked with the moveable feast of Easter. Easter Day is the first Sunday after the first full moon on or after 21 March. If the full moon happens on a Sunday, then Easter Day is the Sunday afterwards. The earliest date for Easter Day is thus 22 March; the latest, 25 April.

The 40 days before Easter are known as Lent and are traditionally a period of fasting, or at least of abstinence from certain foods and pleasures. Ash Wednesday is the first day of Lent. It is preceded by Shrove Tuesday, traditionally a day of some merry-making — a last fling before the long fast. Palm Sunday, the Sunday before Easter, commemorates the triumphal entry of Christ into Jerusalem before his trial and death. Good Friday, the Friday before Easter, commemorates the crucifixion of Christ. Maundy Thursday is the day before Good Friday, the name deriving from the Latin 'mandate' and referring to the command of Christ to his disciples to love one another. All of these church festivals and their religious significance were familiar to our rural ancestors and may well have meant more to them than to us.

The aspect of Shrove Tuesday best remembered today is the traditional making of pancakes. For many people it is Pancake Day and nothing more. The custom arose through the necessity of using up any foodstuffs which were forbidden in Lent. Meat was certainly included, and some writers assert that the ban also applied to eggs and butter, though that would seem not very logical, as eggs are one of the few foods the supply of which tends to increase towards the end of winter, as the hens start laying in response to the increasing day length. However, the practice could have been an indirect method of ensuring a crop of chicken for the coming year, for, with a ban on egg-eating in force, all fresh eggs would be set under broody hens to hatch around Easter-tide. Katharine Briggs, in *The Folklore of the Cotswolds* (1974), suggests that all eggs left over on Shrove Tuesday were hard-boiled, the prohibition being on the eating of fresh eggs. The word 'Shrove' refers to the practice of confessing of sins, after which presumably the fast of Lent could be considered a penance for faults committed.

As with other festivals, Shrove Tuesday was used as an excuse for processions around the villages, demanding alms from the better-off. In more recent times, the processions were confined mainly to children. In many districts the rhymes chanted on these occasions have been preserved, and most of them refer to food. Here are two from Wiltshire:

> A-shrovin', a-shrovin',
> I be come a-shrovin';
> A piece of bread, a piece of cheese,
> A bit of your fat bacon,
> Or a dish of dough-nuts,
> All of your own makin'!

> A-shrovin', a-shrovin',
> Nice meat in a pie,
> My mouth is very dry.

Then there is this one from Warminster:

> Dame, is your pan hot?
>   Lard and corn is dear;
> I've come a-shrovin',
>   Tis but once a year.
> So up to the flitch
> And cut a gurt stitch;
> If your hens don't lay,
> I'll steal your cock away
>   Afore next Shrove Tuesday.

In West Somerset the usual verse was:

> Tippety-Tippety-tin;
> Give me a pancake and I'll come in.
> Tippety-tippety-toe,
> Give me a pancake and then I'll go.

The implied threat was emphasised in the Cornish version:

> Nicky, nicky, nan,
> Give me a pancake and then I'll be
>   gone.
> But if you give me none,
> I'll throw a great stone
> And down your door shall come.

Traditional Shrove Tuesday celebrations were certainly boisterous and sometimes violent. In many districts the custom of 'lensharding' is remembered. The boys and youths who went around demanding alms armed themselves with a good stock of broken crockery, with which they bombarded the door of anyone who refused them. 'Lenshard' is an abbreviation of 'Lent shard' — broken crockery thrown in Lent. On Exmoor and in some other places the custom was observed on Collop Monday, the day before Shrove Tuesday. Sometimes the crocks were shot in at any door left unlocked on the evening of Collop Monday, without the option of buying off the intruders with a pancake or other food. In Cornwall the youngsters banged on doors with clubs and ran away before anyone came out.

In Cornwall, Sussex and elsewhere Shrove Tuesday was a traditional occasion for both cock-fighting and a deplorable sport known as cock-throwing. In the latter, weighted sticks were thrown at a tethered cock. The winner was the thrower who knocked the cock out and grabbed it before it recovered consciousness. In *The Folklore of Sussex* (1973) Jacqueline Simpson describes a Brighton variant of the sport, in which a cock was placed in a large earthenware pot suspended about 16 feet above a narrow street. Contestants were allowed four shies with a heavy stick for twopence, and the cock was awarded to whoever broke the pot.

A custom known as 'Thrashing the Hen' is also recorded for Sussex. All but one of the participants in this sport were blindfolded and armed with sticks. The odd man out was the Hoodman, who had bells tied to his coat-tails and carried a hen in a sack. The blindfolded men had to try to beat the hen to death, but that hardly ever happened, though both the Hoodman and the contestants took plenty of hard knocks. In the Cotswolds hens which had not been laying well were whipped on this day.

In Cornwall Shrove Tuesday was the traditional date for hurling matches. Unlike Irish hurling, in which the ball is hit with a stick, Cornish hurling is more like street football. It is still engaged in annually, and with much ceremony, in St Columb. The game is played through the streets, the goals being two miles apart at opposite ends of the town, and virtually no holds are barred. Wise shopkeepers board up their windows. Similar versions of street football are played in a number of Midland and northern towns. Christina Hole *(English Custom and Usage,* 1941) mentions Ashbourne, Atherstone, Alnwick, Corfe Castle, Chester-le-Street and Sedgefield in this connection. *Chambers' Book of Days* (1864) quotes similar games in Finsbury Fields (London), Teddington and Scone (Perth). In some northern counties Shrove Tuesday used to be considered a general 'Mischief Day', when it was held that one could get away with virtually anything in the way of horse-play.

A less violent custom associated with Shrove Tuesday in many parts of the country is egg-shackling. Eggs, marked with the names of their owners, are placed in a sieve which is then shaken gently till only one is left whole. Its owner is the winner. A variant of the game is to knock eggs together, after the manner of children playing conkers. Another traditional Shrove Tuesday sport still practised in some places, in some instances after a modern revival, is the Pancake Race.

3 Street Football, Corfe Castle, Dorset, 1938

Women race with pancakes in frying-pans, tossing them as they run.

An old custom which seems to have nothing to do with any of the above but which is associated with Shrove Tuesday is clipping the church. Parishioners or school children join hands in the churchyard and encircle the church. Hymns or songs are sung, and in some places a dance was performed. In most places this is now an obsolete custom but in a few it has been revived. Although most often linked with Shrove Tuesday it was not necessarily so. Edward Hutton *(Highways and Byways in Somerset,* 1924) says that at Langford Budville, in that county, it was observed on 29 June and at Wellington on Midsummer Day. Kingsley Palmer *(The Folklore of Somerset,* 1976) considers that the purpose, as with many other customs of this season, was to drive out the devil in preparation for Lent and Easter, but it has also been held to be a relic of a pagan custom, in which worshippers danced around a sacred stone.

Ash Wednesday, the first day of Lent, was a solemn occasion, deriving its name from the ancient practice of blessing ashes, the priest using the occasion to remind his congregation that they too must return to ashes. Kingsley Palmer *(The Folklore of Somerset,* 1976) says that in that county it was known as 'Cussing Day', referring to the custom described by John Brand *(Observations on Popular Antiquities,* 1900) as 'reading publicly on this day the curses denounced against impenitent sinners, when the people are directed to repeat an Amen at the end of each malediction'. Kingsley Palmer comments that people considered this 'tantamount to cursing your neighbour' and doubtless enjoyed the exercise.

In some districts a figure of sticks and straw was made by boys on this day and used as an Aunt Sally, as a poor substitute for the now-defunct cocks. And Jacqueline Simpson *(The Folklore of Sussex,* 1973) says that in that county Ash Wednesday was the traditional date for the opening of the season for playing marbles, which was there considered a sport for adults and the subject of a championship which ended in a grand climax on Good Friday. Other Lenten games, beginning on Ash Wednesday, were tip-cat, bat-and-trap and skipping. Miss Simpson also learned that on Ash Wednesday children should not wear or show anything white, not even a handkerchief.

In early times, when the Lenten fast was strictly observed, there was a huge demand at this season for fish, which were permissible food. Mediaeval accounts for royal and noble households reveal items for enormous quantities of both sea and freshwater fish — herring, stock-fish (cod), eels and conger eels being among those commonly mentioned. Lampreys, those sucker-equipped fish which are parasitic on salmon and for which we have little regard today, were in high favour. King John put a ceiling on their price, fixing it at not more than two shillings each (a colossal price) when the season opened. He once fined the city of Gloucester for failing to provide enough lampreys for his table. Our ancestors were, however, unknowingly inconsistent, for they cheerfully ate the meat of whales, porpoises, seals and dolphins, believing them to be fish.

The one relief from the austerities of Lent was Mid-Lent Sunday, traditionally known as Mothering Sunday. It normally falls in March and is currently enjoying a new popularity, largely commercially inspired, as Mother's Day. Some controversy exists as to whether that was its original significance. Although eighteenth-century writers (quoted by John Brand in *Observations on Popular Antiquities,* 1900) testify to the practice in some parts of the country for 'servants and apprentices to visit their parents and make them a present of money, a trinket or some nice eatable', some authorities think that the 'mother' referred to is Mother Church. The day would thus be an occasion when those who had moved away revisited the church where they had been baptized, and, incidentally, the members of their family who were still residing in the neighbourhood.

Shropshire and Herefordshire have a traditional sweetmeat for Mothering Sunday — Simnel cakes, which have the crust coloured with saffron and which are filled with a rich plum-cake mixture, including plenty of candied peel. In Hampshire the Mothering Sunday cake is less elaborate, being a kind of biscuit or wafer, made of batter and cooked in special tongs held over a hot wood fire. The compilers of the Hampshire Federation of Women's Institutes' book, *It Happened in Hampshire* (1937), record that at Chilbolton these wafers

'have been made every Mid-Lent by a family named Baverstock for at least 200 years, the recipe for mixing the batter being a secret which passes from mother to daughter-in-law, together with the wafer irons . . . . The wafers were originally (as one theory has it) baked in the neighbouring monastery and distributed to the worshippers after Holy Communion, as a memento of the Feast.'

Be that as it may, early in the nineteenth century the blacksmith at Odstock, in Wiltshire, had a similar set of irons which he used for making 'pat-a-cakes' for the children who came to his forge (as recalled in my book, *The Folklore of Wiltshire,* 1976).

In the north of England a dish, known as carlings, was made of peas fried in butter and well seasoned with pepper and salt and was eaten on this Sunday or the following one. In the midlands and south its place was taken by a frumety, in which boiled wheat grains in milk, with sugar and spice, were the chief ingredients.

Whatever the fare, Mid-Lent Sunday was a brief but welcome respite from the hardships of the season. Ernest Marwick *(The Folkore of Orkney and Shetland,* 1975) says that in those northern islands it was known as the *Lang Reid* — the long period of hard weather. In the Faroes, he adds, the children dress in sheepskins on the first Monday in Lent to represent a monster who comes down from the mountains 'to cut out the stomachs of children who are crying for meat in Lent'.

Lent, which commonly embraces much of the month of March, is, although often a season of unpleasant weather, one of the most important seasons of the year in the farming calendar. It is the time when the efficient farmer is busy with the sowing of his crops. Above all else, he values dry, cold weather, such as often occurs in late February and March. ' A peck of dust in March is worth a king's ransom', is still an oft-quoted proverb and is accurate enough. Another reminds us that 'Well sown is half-grown'.

The main spring-sown cereal in England and Wales today is barley, but oats, too, benefit from early sowing, even as early as January, as the following verse indicates:

Who in January sows oats
Gets gold and groats;
Who sows in May
Gets little that way.

Yet another agricultural proverb on the same theme declares that, 'the early man never borrows from the late man.' And 'A dry March never begs its bread.'

The proverb-makers are not so sure about February. One farming adage asserts that

If in February there be no rain
Tis neither good for hay nor grain.

But most arable farmers can make good use of a dry February. Incidentally, though February is notoriously associated with floods, as in the appellation 'February fill-dyke', it is statistically one of the driest months of the year.

As so often happens, many old country beliefs are not content with generalities but strive to be more precise. A well-known proverb is:

So many mists in March,
So many frosts in May.

Whether or not it has any validity, it is nonsense, as I have heard it claimed, to say that because 5 March, for example, is misty, 5 May will be frosty.

The Shepherd's Almanack for 1676 records one similar old-time belief: 'some say Thunder on Shrove Tuesday fortelleth wind, store of fruit and plenty. Others affirm that so much as the sun shineth that day, the like will shine every day in Lent.'

*   *   *

Seedtime in Britain is always a period of hard work and anxiety. The growing season in our high northern latitudes is short enough under the most favourable circumstances, and every farmer and gardener is eager to prolong it as far as possible by getting his seeds sown early. Farmers in my part of the country (south-western England) say that for every day that barley-sowing is delayed after 14 April the yield will decline by a hundredweight per acre. That, I am sure, is an exaggeration, much depending on the subsequent weather, but the general inference is accurate enough. As we have already noted, the sort of weather appreciated by agriculturists in March is that which produces dust. Unfortunately for the comfort of the sower, the type of weather most likely to have that effect is an anticyclone bringing cold north-easters across the North Sea. The discomfort is a price which the dedicated husbandman will gladly pay for an early seedtime.

As though catching favourable weather were not difficult enough, our ancestors imposed yet another obstacle. They considered that nearly all seeds, the exceptions being beans and peas, had to be sown when the moon was waxing. The thinking behind the belief seems to have been that as the moon became full so the seeds expanded and grew, in accordance with a kind of sympathetic magic.

Recent investigations suggest that the idea may not be so ridiculous after all. It has long been established that the moon is responsible for the ocean tides, and now it has been demonstrated that every drop of water on our planet is similarly affected. As all living bodies are composed largely of water, all life responds to the rhythm of the moon. When the moon is full and the tides are at their zenith, certain types of insanity reach their peak, as also does the incidence of haemorrhages among patients particularly susceptible to bleeding. In 1962 the American magazine *Science* published the results of meticulous investigations conducted independently by scientists in the United States and Australia which showed conclusively that rainfall tended to be heaviest 'near the middle of the first and third weeks of the synodical month'. And the American researcher, F.A. Brown *(Nature,* 211, 1966), has compiled enormous masses of data to show that potatoes respond to the fluctuations in the lunar period.

It would therefore seem entirely logical that seeds should be similarly affected, and that the ancient beliefs were founded, in the first place, on accurate observation. But why the germination of peas and beans should be associated with the waning moon, while that of all other seeds was linked with the waxing moon, has yet to be explained.

*   *   *

Both Wales and Ireland have patron saints whose feast days fall in Lent. St David's Day is 1 March; St Patrick's, 17 March. St David's Day has a certain agricultural significance. Apparently, if any small farmer had, through illness or other misfortune, failed to get his land ploughed by this date, his neighbours rallied round to help him. They came to the farm with their ploughs and oxen, and their wives accompanied them, to cook for the entire company. As food was scarce by that time of the year, leeks were a welcome addition to the communal stock-pot, and every housewife brought her quota.

CHAPTER 4

The Coming of Spring

ALMOST INVARIABLY, for a brief period of March winter temporarily abdicates and the countryside enjoys a false summer, in which the temperature often rises to above 70°F. The duration of this welcome respite may be a week or ten days, after which winter returns. It is fortunate when, as sometimes happens, this cheering foretaste of spring coincides with Easter. I have vivid memories of one such spring when I was a boy. Even my father, who was normally far too busy for such idleness, went with us all to the woods and spent Good Friday afternoon picking primroses, violets and wood anemones. Song-thrushes and chaffinches were singing; brimstone butterflies were flitting around, as though they were primroses that had broken loose from their anchoring stems; a whispering which filled the woods was made by little black wolf-spiders, scampering over a carpet of dead beech leaves; queen bumble-bees were on the wing, looking for the nesting-site where they would establish a summer colony; fluffy white clouds floating across a pale blue sky spoke of more fine weather to come.

After such an experience, though winter is sure to close in again, it never seems quite as bad as before. We know that real spring, of which we have just enjoyed a sample, cannot be long delayed.

The very number of feast days which cluster around Easter is an indication of how glad people must have been that the lean days of Lent and winter were ending. The chief red-letter days in the calendar were Palm Sunday; then Good Friday and Easter-tide; then, a week later, Hock-tide; and, somewhere in between, on the fixed date of 1 April, April Fools' Day. All, even Good Friday with its sombre recollections of the Crucifixion, provided at least some respite from the ordinary and wearisome routine of Lent. Good Friday's contribution was hot cross buns, which are still baked and sold on that day.

4 Giving Pax Cakes at
King's Caple,
Herefordshire

Palm Sunday, which is the Sunday before Easter Day, commemorates Jesus's triumphal ride on a donkey into Jerusalem. The crowd tore branches from the palm trees and strewed them before him. In England we have no palms, so convention has substituted the sallow, or 'pussy willow', which is in bloom at this season and which is called 'palm' in many districts. Formerly 'palm' branches were carried in procession to church on Palm Sunday; nowadays in many churches 'palm' provides the chief floral decorations for that day (though some clergy will allow no flowers at all in their churches before Easter Day).

Palm Sunday processions and the attendant festivities were among the ancient religious customs to which the early Protestants were vigorously opposed. Brand *(Observations on Popular Antiquities,* 1900) quotes a seventeenth-century Protestant protagonist, a Dr Fulke:

> 'Your Palm Sunday procession was horrible idolatry, and abusing the Lord's Institution, who ordained his Supper to be eaten and drunken, not to be carried about in procession like a heathenish idol; but it is pretty sport that you make the Priests that carry this idol to supply the room of the Ass on which Christ did ride. Thus you turn the holy mystery of Christ's riding to Jerusalem to a May-game and pageant-play.'

From which one may gather that some at least of the celebrations associated with Palm Sunday resembled those of May Day. And Jacqueline Simpson *(The Folklore of Sussex,* 1973) quotes a newspaper report of April 1831, to the effect that on Palm Sunday the peace had been disturbed by

> 'hundreds of people of both sexes who, on the excuse of ''going a-palming'', had come out from Brighton and spent the whole day in breaking down and gathering all the willows and withies in the hedges that were covered with yellow flowers. In the evening they went to the local inn; here they drank excessively, so that the night ended with many brawls.'

Wiltshire seems to have had a tradition of Palm Sunday fairs, none of which now survives, though some lingered in the memories of old people as late as the 1930s. All were held on chalk hill-tops. When collecting material for my *Folklore of Wiltshire* I found references and recollections of no fewer than six such fairs. A common feature of most of them was the playing of a game called 'bandy', in which a ball was hit to the top of the hill by men and boys armed with curved sticks and stationed in an oblique line from base to summit. Sliding down the steep slopes was also popular, and it is recorded that on Martinsell Hill, near Pewsey, the boys used the jawbones of horses as toboggans.

The villagers of Avebury preserved the custom of walking in procession on Palm Sunday to the top of Silbury Hill, that gigantic man-made pyramid of chalk and soil which is a continuing enigma to archaeologists. There they used to 'eat fig cakes and drink sugar and water'. On Bidcombe Hill, near Maiden Bradley, country people kept up the tradition of eating 'furmety' on Palm Sunday, as they sat around a depression on the hillside, known as 'Furmety Hole'. Furmety is a kind of wheaten porridge, and something similar was eaten on the same date at Swallowhead Springs, one of the sources of the Kennet in north Wiltshire. Water from the springs was mixed with sugar, and fig cake provided the solid part of the meal.

It is significant that food comprises an important feature of these festivals, coming towards the end of the austere period of Lent. Also that the food was, to our palates, somewhat plain and uninteresting, there being little variety left at that season of the year. In the Cotswolds Palm Sunday was sometimes known as Fig Pudding Day, the figs probably referring to raisins.

In Somerset hill-top celebrations, similar to those observed in Wiltshire on Palm Sunday, were transferred to Good Friday. Here too the custom of proceeding to a certain hollow in a high hill — Brent Knoll — for what had become a picnic is recorded (by Kingsley Palmer, *The Folklore of Somerset*, 1976). There are memories of Good Friday fairs from several parts of the country. Cornwall had one at Perranporth; Cambridgeshire one on Bartlow Hills, which was attended by the villagers of Linton and Hadstock.

Those of us who can remember our primary schooldays will recall that there were set seasons for certain games and sports. We played them assiduously for a few weeks and then discarded them till the next year. Skipping was a springtime sport, and folklore links it, in some places, with Good Friday. Enid Porter *(Cambridgeshire Customs and Folklore*, 1969) says that those villagers of Linton and Hadstock who went to Bartlow Hills on Good Friday skipped there. The people of Cambridge used to go to a traditional place, Parker's Piece, and there skip all day, with breaks for snack meals which they brought with them. Whole families attended, and usually it was the women who did the skipping, the men turning the rope. The custom was kept up until the Second World War. A similar custom was popular in Sussex, especially at Brighton, and lasted until the same interruption by war. Long skipping ropes, generally clothes'-lines, over which several persons could skip together, were used. In Sussex, too, Good Friday was, and is, the date that marks the ending of the marble-playing season (see above) and was even known in some districts as Marble Day. All games had to cease by the stroke of noon. Jacqueline Simpson *(The Folklore of Sussex*, 1973) quotes the vicar of Selmeston in 1879 to the effect that people who would never dream of playing marbles at any other time would do so on Good Friday. In both Sussex and Cambridgeshire an alternative name for Good Friday was Long Rope Day, because of the length of the rope used for skipping. At Hove the Good Friday games and associated festivities were linked with a prehistoric burial mound just outside the town. The tumulus has since, unfortunately, been demolished.

The customs associated with Good Friday are curiously contradictory. On the one hand we have these games, sports, fairs and general merry-making; on the other, sundry taboos connected with a particularly solemn religious anniversary. The first probably have the deeper roots, referring to the general sense of gladness associated with seedtime and the coming of spring.

As noted on page 11, Good Friday has a special significance in the gardener's calendar. It is the day divinely ordained for the planting of potatoes, according to West Country lore, from Cornwall to Wiltshire. On Exmoor it used to be considered that seed sown at midday on Good Friday would have double flowers. Among the seeds specially mentioned for sowing on this day was parsley, which is supposed to germinate very capriciously, though I have never found it so. Anyhow, all possible difficulties will be banished by sowing the seed on Good Friday; the seedlings will come up without delay, and the leaves will all be curly. It is curious that the superstitions about planting potatoes should be so widespread (they are found in many counties) in view of the fact that the potato has been widely cultivated in Britain for less than 300 years. Presumably Good Friday was found to be a convenient day for the planting, at a time when weekends were not regarded as holidays, and the customs thus begun soon absorbed traditions formerly associated with other plants and seeds. On the other hand, in some places it is considered wrong to work on Good Friday. In parts of Cambridgeshire farm workers had a holiday on that day, provided they went to church in the morning. Cornish fishermen refused to put to sea, and in west Somerset housewives refused to do their washing.

The custom of eating hot cross buns on Good Friday is said to derive from the former practice of making cakes from the dough from which the sacramental bread was also made, for eating on Good Friday. It was traditional to eat the buns for breakfast, and so vendors were on the streets very early, shouting their wares with rhymes, the commonest of which was:

> *Hot cross buns!*
> *Hot cross buns!*
> *One a penny, two a penny,*
> *Hot cross buns!*
> *If you have no daughters,*
> *Give them to your sons.*
> *One a penny, two a penny,*
> *Hot cross buns!*

Hot cross buns, which are still made in many parts of the country (though not delivered in time for breakfast!), are, of course, spiced and usually contain a few currants, but in the past many housewives used to mark the batches of bread they baked on Good Friday with a cross. Such loaves, it was said, would keep fresh in a tin for a whole year, and in Cambridgeshire it was a tradition to moisten them and eat them at tea-time on Easter Day. Those who received a slice bearing a part of the cross on the crust could look forward to a lucky year. Such bread would never go mouldy and, when crumbled and powdered, was considered a good remedy for indigestion.

The day before Good Friday is Maundy Thursday, a day now little regarded except insofar as the annual distribution of Maundy Money is usually recorded by the Press. Maundy is derived from the Latin mandate, referring to Christ's command to his disciples to love one another, a command which he demonstrated

by washing his disciples' feet. In the past the kings of England used to wash the feet of poor men, to a number equal to the number of years in their reign. James II is said to have been the last monarch to observe the custom. More recently it has been commuted to a gift of specially-minted money, distributed by the monarch on this day to a number of ordinary citizens who have served their community well.

The day was also once known as Shear Thursday, because on it men cut their hair and trimmed their beards, which had presumably been left unkempt all through Lent.

*   *   *

Etymologically, Easter commemorates the Saxon goddess, Eostre, whose festival was celebrated at this season. The original Saxon name for April was Eosturmonath. Early Christians called it the Paschal festival, from its association with the Jewish Passover, and the name still survives in parts of England in the term 'Pace egg' for Easter egg.

Pace eggs, or Easter eggs, are cardboard or chocolate replicas of real eggs, replacing the hard-boiled eggs dyed in various bright colours which were in vogue until comparatively recent times. Eggs are, of course, at their most plentiful around Easter and are an appropriate symbol of resurrection — new life emerging

5 Good Friday loaves, at Aymestrey, Herefordshire

from the dark womb of winter. Moreover, in mediaeval times, where so many of our customs have their roots, eggs were restored to their place in the menu at Easter, after the Lenten fast.

Eggs feature in the traditional Easter Monday sports of many places. A widespread custom was egg-rolling, in which hard-boiled eggs were rolled down grassy slopes. It seems likely that the object was to keep one's egg intact for as long as possible and, in some versions, to guide it through a goal at the bottom of the hill. The custom was more widespread in Lancashire, Yorkshire and the north than in southern and midland counties. In parts of Lancashire it was associated with the usual procession of children to houses, demanding gifts on the pretext that they were 'pace-egging'. And in the same county folklorists have retrieved recollections of a Pace-egging Play, apparently on the lines of Christmas mumming plays.

In the southern counties one comes across widespread references to a belief that if one rose very early on Easter Day and climbed to the top of the nearest high hill one could see the sun dance. I have heard of it in Cornwall, Devon, Somerset and Sussex. On Exmoor it was also held that, with luck, a lamb could be seen silhouetted against the disc of the rising sun — the obvious association being with the Paschal Lamb. But the Devil generally thwarted the hopes of the young men and girls who climbed the hills so early in the morning, either by conjuring up a bank of clouds or by magically raising the height of distant hills, so that the sun could not be seen until it was too late.

A common village custom until the late eighteenth or early nineteenth centuries was the holding of Church Ales, which were simply village feasts. Often the drinks and victuals were traditionally provided by the parson, which caused much friction between him and his parishioners, each new incumbent trying to stop a custom which must have been a severe drain on his purse while his flock were equally adamant in preserving their alleged right to a free meal. It seems that in the end the parsons won, for few if any Church Ales survive. The season to which they applied varied from parish to parish, but in many places they were held at Easter. One which was associated with Easter was held at Chisledon, near Swindon, concerning which Mr F.A. Carrington wrote in the *Wiltshire Archaeological Magazine* in 1852, that,

'I was told in the year 1838 . . . that on Easter Tuesday in every year the clerk of the parish of Chisledon had an ale; which was effected by the clerk providing a good plain dinner and plenty of strong beer, at his house, for the principal parishioners to partake of; this was called the Clerk's Ale, for which each guest made the clerk a present.'

This would seem to be a sensible arrangement, for without it there would have been very little competition for the post of parish clerk.

Other Wiltshire parishes had vestiges of ancient traditions of ceremonies attached to Ales, especially those held in spring. They had to do with garlands of flowers, draped around the necks of the chief participants, and in one instance (at

Ogbourne St George) there was an association with two tumuli on a hill in the neighbourhood.

One of the best-known Easter Monday customs is that of the hare-pie scramble and bottle-kicking match at Hallaton, in Leicestershire. The pies are now made of beefsteak, hares being out of season, but otherwise the custom still follows its traditional course. The rector of Hallaton divides the large pies, which have been baked in his kitchen and tosses the slices to the crowds of people who assemble to scramble for them on his lawn.

After the game is over, the bottle-kicking match begins. The bottle is not a glass one but a miniature wooden cask, of the sort known as 'plough-bottles' which workmen formerly carried to the fields with their daily ration of ale or cider. The contest is between the men of Hallaton and those of the neighbouring parish of Medbourne, the latter reinforced by anyone else who cares to join in. The object is to kick the little barrel over the brook which marks the boundary of the parishes. There are very few if any rules, and the game is decidedly vigorous. Afterwards a much larger barrel of beer is broached on the village green and shared by victors and vanquished alike.

6 Preparing for the Bottle-kicking Match at Hallaton, Leicestershire

Christina Hole (*English Custom and Usage*, 1941) suggests that the bottle-

kicking event may be a survival of an ancient ceremony symbolising the chasing away of winter by spring, and so it may, but it almost certainly owes its survival to the opportunity it provided for the inhabitants of two neighbouring villages to work off their antagonisms. Intense rivalry between two adjacent communities is very common, and bottle-kicking is one of many safety-valves.

As for the hare-pie, vestiges of similar ceremonies have been traced in other Midland parishes. Christina Hole records that at Coleshill, in Warwickshire, a hare had to be caught and presented, live, to the parson before ten o'clock in the morning of Easter Day. In return, he had to give the donors a hundred eggs, a calf's head and a groat. At one time the Mayor and Corporation of Leicester, in full regalia, used to go to a spot on the Dane hills on Easter Monday 'to hunt the hare'. Hares were sacred animals to the pre-Christian Celts. Later, when the old gods came to be regarded, by pious Christians, as devils, hares were associated with witchcraft. Customs which feature hares would therefore seem to offer direct links with a pagan past. And, of course, the old traditions would be kept fresh in people's minds each spring by the spectacular behaviour of 'mad March Hares' at mating time.

In addition to Easter eggs, Easter has a traditional sweetmeat in 'Easter cakes'. These are round, flat cakes with scalloped edges, containing spices and currants and sprinkled with sugar. They were an essential part of Easter in my boyhood home in Wiltshire in the 1920s and are, I think, still widely available today. In some districts 'tansy cakes', so-called because tansy is one of the main herbs used for flavouring, are made, but these seem to be rather different from Easter cakes and, at least in the original version, were intended to be eaten with a meat dish, much as Yorkshire pudding is.

Certain other Easter ceremonies are confined to single places or groups of places. For instance, Lostwithiel, in Cornwall, used in times past to stage an impressive banquet at which one of the citizens was royally entertained as a 'mock prince'. Penzance had a traditional Easter game, 'lilly-bangers', played with dice. The people of Leafield, in Oxfordshire, claimed to have the right to enter Wychwood Forest on Easter Monday in order to collect water from sacred springs there. This water they mixed with liquorice and then bottled as tonic for all manner of ailments. At Ashton-under-Lyne, in Lancashire, an Easter Monday procession featuring a 'black knight' paraded around the town, after which the effigy of the knight was smashed to pieces.

In *The Folklore of Orkney and Shetland* (1975) Ernest Marwick describes a peculiar ceremony held originally at Easter on the island of South Ronaldshay, Orkney. The small girls and some of the small boys go to a beach and plough the sand. The children are dressed in scintillating costumes in which the various items of a horse's harness, such as collars, shoes, bridle, tail and horse-brasses, are featured, and prizes are awarded for the best outfit. The beach to be ploughed is of damp sand, and judging takes serious account of the straightness and evenness of the furrows, just as in an ordinary ploughing-match. The festival concludes with tea, games and dancing. It is known as The Festival of the Horse and has now been transferred to a date in August, for the benefit of tourists who visit the island at that season. Its agricultural significance, in relation to the country calendar, is thus obscured, but the custom would seem to be related to those connected, farther south, with Plough Monday.

In spite of the diverse Easter customs of which those described above are a sample, there are many places in Britain which have no Easter traditions at all, apart from the usual church services. For Easter church-going it has become a tradition for women to wear their new spring outfits. In Victorian times this was typified by a new 'Easter bonnet', but few women wear hats in church today. Within the last two decades the decorating of churches with elaborate flower arrangements has become widespread, doubtless linked with the increasingly popular art of flower arranging.

The Easter Monday cart-horse parade in Regent's Park, London, is of comparatively recent origin, the first having been held in 1886, following the formation of the London Carthorse Parade Society. In 1965 this Society amalgamated with the London Vanhorse Parade Society, which had been holding its parade on Whit Monday, and Easter Monday was then fixed as the date of the combined event. It is now one of the outstanding outdoor events in the London calendar, often attracting 20,000 to 30,000 spectators, and is indeed a superb spectacle, with magnificent teams of huge horses, jingling and glittering in their highly polished regalia, obviously enjoying their day out.

The Monday and the Tuesday of the week following Easter week were formerly celebrated as Hock-tide, a festival largely forgotten, except in a few places where particularly tenacious traditions survive. One such place is Hungerford, in Berkshire, where it is connected with the town's ancient court. Instead of a mayor and corporation, Hungerford has as its governing body a Constable, a Portreeve and Bailiff, and a Court of Feoffees, the last-named consisting of 12 elected members, whose duty is to control common rights, fishing rights and similar matters. The Court meets to do business, hear claims and disputes and to elect a new Constable and officers on the Tuesday of Hock-tide. The meeting is followed by a civic lunch, after which any new commoners have to endure the ordeal of 'Shoeing the Colt'. A 'blacksmith' seizes the newcomer and pretends to hammer nails into the sole of his shoe, until he purchases his immunity by buying a round of drinks.

An essential feature of the Hungerford Hock-tide celebrations is the presence of two Tutti-men, a name thought to derive from 'Tithing-men'. Their first duty on the meeting day is to call on the Constable and escort him to the Town Hall. Then, while the meeting is in progress, they parade around the town, accompanied by an 'Orange Scrambler' and calling at the houses of all the commoners. At each house they demand a coin from every man and a kiss from every woman. Each tutti-man carries a tutti-pole, which is a long pole festooned with ribbons and an orange fixed to the top. When a kiss is given, the tutti-man who receives it presents an orange in exchange. In their search for kisses the tutti-men do not necessarily confine themselves to the town's commoners but make

*7 Tutti-men at the
Hocktide celebrations,
Hungerford, 1937*

their demands on passers-by and even motorists. The tutti-men and orange-scrambler are usually accompanied by a crowd of children and other spectators. At the civic lunch the tutti-men take their places on either side of the newly-elected Constable. Afterwards they go outside with the orange-scrambler, to toss oranges to the waiting children.

Formerly the Hungerford Hock-tide festivities included a supper on the previous evening (the Monday). The menu consisted of black broth, welsh rarebit, macaroni, and watercress salad, washed down with punch.

Hungerford's Hock-tide celebrations are unique, but the village of Tilshead, in Wiltshire, perhaps once had something of the sort, for old parish records refer to 'tutti-men'. Tilshead was once a much larger place than it is at present, being at the time of the Domesday Book one of the largest boroughs in the county. Sixteenth-century records speak of Hock-tide being observed in London and Reading, and it seems to have been popular in the north of England.

The celebration of Hock-tide in the Cotswolds took rather different forms (see Katharine Briggs in *The Folklore of the Cotswolds*, 1974). At Randwick (known locally as 'Runnick') in Gloucestershire a 'mock mayor' was elected and carried through the village with great enthusiasm . . . to the village pond, where he was dumped. The pond being shallow, he continued sitting on his throne while the 'Runnick Weavers' Song' was sung, after which he did his best to drench all his attendants. The occasion was known as 'Runnick Wap' and is still merrily observed, though the date has now been shifted to the first Saturday after May Day, in order to coincide with another Randwick festival, the rolling of three Double Gloucester cheeses around the churchyard. The traditional day for Runnick Wap was the Monday of Hock-tide. It was preceded on the Sunday by a service attended by most of the villagers, at which Numbers, Chapter 22, was read as the lesson. The chapter contains the story of Balaam's Ass, for which reason the day was known locally as Balaam's Ass Day.

Elsewhere in the Cotswolds ropes were slung across village streets in order to exact tolls from passers-by. Hock-Monday was the day reserved for the men; Hock-Tuesday for the women.

Associated with the festival in many northern places was the custom of 'lifting', again practised by men and women on alternate days. On the Monday the young men carried around a decorated chair, knocking at house doors, seizing any woman who answered it and placing her on the chair to be kissed. On the Tuesday it was the turn of the girls to take the initiative. Sometimes the chair was omitted, the victims being lifted bodily in the arms of the aggressors. Christina Hole *(English Custom and Usage,* 1941) refers to the fate of a man in Wednesbury who was 'lifted and kissed till he was black in the face by a party of leather-breeched coal-pit women'!

The origins of Hock-tide are obscure, though it seems to have had an ancient importance, for half-yearly rents were sometimes payable at that date. It was a moveable feast, linked to Easter.

Although apparently having no connection with any other Hock-tide celebrations, Devon had a spring festival which generally coincided with Hock-tide week. It consisted of hare-hunting on Dartmoor, culminating, after a whole week of festivities, in a grand hunt on Bellever Tor; hence the occasion was known as Bellever Day. The Rev. Sabine Baring-Gould, writing in 1899, says that 'all the towns and villages neighbouring on Dartmoor send out carriages, traps, carts, riders; the roads are full of men and women, ay, and children, hurrying to Bellever . . . .'

Turning now to festivals unaffected by the date of Easter, we have a still-popular one in April Fools' Day — 1 April. Or rather, it is a half-day, for traditionally April Fool jokes have to be played before noon, after which the victim was entitled to turn the tables by shouting,

> *April Fool's gone past,*
> *And you're the biggest fool at last.*

At Christow, in Devon, however, pranks had to be played in the afternoon. The day there was known as 'Tail-pipe Day', because it was a custom to pin an inscription 'Please kick me' or something similar to the coat-tails of an unsuspecting victim.

The game was to catch someone unawares. As school-children we used to invite our friends to 'look at that thrush's nest in the hedge there; it's got eggs already', or 'mind! there's a big spider on the wall behind you!' (what child could resist looking round!). More elaborate practical jokes were related by our elders, who told of how a blacksmith (named) was sent on a fool's errand to shoe a horse at a farm two miles away. There were traditional jokes, such as sending an apprentice to a shop to buy a 'packet of hurdle-seed', or 'a half-pint of pigeon's milk', or 'a bottle of strap-oil', the last-named request being met by the shopkeeper's strap laid across the victim's backside.

The origin of April Fool customs is uncertain, though they are certainly widespread throughout much of Europe. A current theory links them with Lud, a Celtic god of humour, whose ancient festival was celebrated around this date. In Scotland the day is known as 'Gowkie Day' or 'Hunt the Gowk', — the 'gowk' being the cuckoo. It is kept up in much the same way. In Orkney, however, many of the pranks are transferred to 2 April, which is known as 'Tailing Day', with associations reminiscent of those of Christow. In addition to joke cards, boys tried to pin pigs'-tails, begged from the butcher, to their comrades' coats or trousers; the more daring, when possible, turning their attention to adults.

Two saints' days in April which have significance in some places are those of St George (23 April) and St Mark (25 April). Flags bearing the red cross of St George fly from church towers on 23 April more frequently than a few decades ago, perhaps indicating a revival of patriotism, at least on the part of parish incumbents.

Norwich is probably the place where St George's Day is remembered with most ceremony, it being normally Mayor's Day, when the newly-elected mayor, aldermen and councillors attend service in the Cathedral. Paradoxically, St George is very much less in evidence than the dragon which he is supposed to have vanquished. The dragon at Norwich is a traditional character named Snap, resplendent in green and gold and with wings of the conventional dragon type, who at other times resides in the Castle Museum. He follows the procession to the Cathedral but has to sit outside on 'the dragon's stone' during the service. He has snapping jaws which can be manipulated by the man inside and causes much merriment as he capers about the streets.

The associations of St Mark's Eve are quite different. This is the night when the ghosts of those who are to die in the following year pass in procession into the church. Whoever stands in the churchyard, at a spot from where he can see the porch, from 11 p.m. to 1 a.m. for three successive years would see the silent spectres. But if he falls asleep and so sees nothing it is supposed that he himself is doomed to die. In East Anglia it was held that those who were to die stayed in the church; the others, who came out again, would have a serious illness during the year but would recover. At Whittlesford, in Cambridgeshire, it was the ghosts who emerged from the church who were to die. They could be seen noting the site

of their future graves in the churchyard.

April sees the arrival in England of the first spring bird migrants, and notably the swallow and the cuckoo. Several counties possess interesting cuckoo lore, Somerset folk being traditionally known as 'Somerset cuckoos'. In Wiltshire, Downton Spring Fair, long since discontinued, used to be held on St George's Day, 23 April. Downton lies in the Avon valley, which here is orientated directly north-south, and Wiltshire villages situated to the north used to say that Downton Fair day was the day 'when they opened the gates at Downton to let the cuckoo through'. Another version says that the people of Downton shut the cuckoo in the pound and were surprised when it escaped by flying out over the enclosing fence.

At Mere, in the south-west corner of Wiltshire, there used to be a 'Cuckowe King', apparently elected annually to preside at a 'Church Ale' about this season. And the folklore of Somerset is full of references to cuckoo pennings.

Books have been written about this curious little branch of folklore. One theory advanced is that the 'cuckoo' in many of the old traditions is not the bird but the Britons of the Dark Ages. These Celts were derisively termed 'cuckoos', meaning nincompoops, by the advancing Saxons, largely because they were too stupid to understand the Saxon language, as any normally bright person would do with ease! The 'cuckoo pen' legends usually refer to places of ancient origin with at least the traces of a fortified earthwork, so it can be assumed that this was where the invaders managed to get those British cuckoos penned. But sometimes, of course, the penned cuckoos managed to break out or escape. An interesting account of the theory and of the incidence of cuckoo lore is to be found in *The Myth of the Pent Cuckoo,* by the Rev. J. E. Field (1913).

Throughout this chapter we have referred to Easter and the associated festivals as being characterised by rejoicing at the coming of spring, and rightly so. Spring had indeed arrived. The flowers were opening, the young lambs were being dropped, the wild birds were singing and nesting, the short British summer was only just ahead. But spring is a fickle season. April is sometimes one of the harshest months of the year, made more cruel and frustrating by the unwelcome lingering of winter when the warm summer sunshine is so near. In March we usually have a foretaste of summer, as already mentioned, but inevitably it is followed by a relapse into wintry conditions. One of the most reliable features of weather lore is the intrusion of a 'blackthorn winter', towards the end of April, when the blackthorn is in bloom. I remember that some years ago, in the 1950s I think, I used as a Christmas card a photograph taken in the previous year in my Wiltshire village. It was one of those sentimental snow scenes which one associates with Christmas, with thatched cottages wearing a thick greatcoat of snow and with icicles hanging from the eaves. But it had been taken not on 25 December but on 25 April.

Typical of mid-April weather are small puffy white clouds floating on a cold, north-easterly breeze over frost-stricken fields. Farmers have been heard to complain bitterly: 'Just as soon as we get the sowing finished and the seed needs warm rain to start it growing, we hit one of these winter droughts.' Manx farmers have a saying, 'As lasting as the parching winds of Spring.'

Many country proverbs carry a similar message, warning of the dangers of being deceived by the early signs of spring:

> *From Christmas to May*
> *Weak cattle decay.*

Note that it is not until May that any improvement can be reckoned on.

'In spring, hair is worth more than meat.' This means that no-one can expect a fat animal in spring but that one which has survived the winter with a thick coat is likely to do well in the coming summer.

> *When the cuckoo sings on an empty bough*
> *Keep your hay and sell your cow.*

The empty bough is one without leaves, and one which is in that state by the time the cuckoo arrives indicates a late and backward spring. There will be little spring grass available.

> *If apples bloom in March*
> *In vain you'll for them search;*
> *If apples bloom in April*
> *Why then they'll be plentiful;*
> *If apples bloom in May*
> *You may eat them night and day.*

Not quite accurate, for an unseasonable frost in May can ruin the apple crop for the year. But the warning is valid enough. Early blooms run greater hazards from frosts.

A rhyme, applicable to this season, which attempts to forecast the weather in the coming summer, is still widely known:

> *If the ash comes out before the oak,*
> *Then we'll surely have a soak.*
> *If the oak comes out before the ash,*
> *Then we'll only have a splash.*

It sounds reasonable, but, casting back deep into my memory, I cannot remember a year when the oak unfolded its leaves, or its flowers, before the ash!

CHAPTER 5

May Day and Morris Men

Ne'er cast a clout
Till May is out,

THIS WAS a rhyme often repeated by solicitous parents in the village of my boyhood, but we were never sure whether the May referred to was the month of May or the hawthorn blossom, which we called May. So we continued to wear our pullovers and flannel vests and thick pants and similar protective clothing until at least towards the end of the month of May. Which fulfilled the purpose of the proverb in reminding us that, even now the long-desired month of May had been reached, spring was still fickle and that it was never safe to trust spring weather.

Quite severe frosts have been known in May, even in the south of England. In Devon 19, 20 and 21 May were once known as Frankimass, the feast of St Frankan, — a saint, incidentally, unknown in any other hagiology. As St Frankan seems to have been synonymous with the Devil, that is hardly surprising. According to one version of the story, Frankan was a Devonshire brewer who was meeting with such severe competition from cider-makers that he sold his soul to the Devil in return for a guarantee of a frost every year on those three days in May, when the apple trees would be in full bloom. Another version says that as part of the bargain the Devonshire brewers had to agree to adulterate their ale, so when May frosts come it is a sign that the brewers have been keeping their word and calling upon the Devil to keep his.

It sounds like a popular bit of anti-brewer propaganda, inspired by Devon cider-makers, but the salient fact is that in most years frosts are to be expected when the apple blossom is out. Fruit farmers have to install elaborate and expensive devices to protect their crops and think themselves lucky when they don't have to use them.

For all that, all over Europe May Day has from very ancient times been celebrated as a spring festival. By 1 May spring obviously has arrived, despite occasional lapses subsequently. The air is filled with bird song; swallows have returned to nest in the barns; bluebells, primroses and wood anemones are carpeting the woods; and every meadow testifies to the fact that 'when you can put your foot on nine daisies at once, spring has come'. (It is also worth bearing in mind that before the change in the calendar in 1752 May Day fell 11 days later, and spring would then be even further advanced.)

In their origins May Day celebrations may be taken as spontaneous rejoicing over the end of winter and the coming of spring. To our ancestors everything around them in the countryside spoke of growth and fertility. The newly-sown seed was sprouting. New-born lambs were in the meadows, newly-hatched chicks in the farmyard. New leaves were appearing on the trees. Bees were laying the foundations of new swarms. Birds everywhere were mating and nesting. What could be more natural than for humans to join in?

By Old May Day at least it was warm enough to spend the nights out-of-doors, in the greenwood. So to the woods the young men and girls went gaily, eager to participate in the rites of the renewal of life. And in the morning they brought back with them green boughs freshly bursting into leaf, as tokens that they had identified themselves with the revival of nature which was proceeding so exuberantly all around. Virtually all the May Day customs and traditions, still surviving or remembered, have this basis. Some have slipped a little away from the traditional date and have attached themselves to other days in May, or even in June, as we shall see in later chapters. Even the maypole is a phallic symbol, and was recognised as such by the grave and intolerant Puritans, who strove hard to suppress May Day festivities.

In my native Wiltshire village little notice was taken of May Day itself, what survived of the old customs having been transferred to Whitsuntide, and that seems to have been true of most Wiltshire villages. The only reference I knew was the song, sung as a round:

> *May Day's breaking,*
> *All the world's awaking,*
> *Let me see the sun rise*
> *Over the Plain.*
>
> *Why have you awoke me?*
> *How you do provoke me!*
> *Let me have a little time to doze off again.*
>
> *Sleeping in the daytime,*
> *Wastes the happy May-time*
> *Makes an empty pocket and a cloudy brain.*

*9 Magdalen College
Choir singing the
traditional Latin hymns
on the top of Magdalen
College tower on May
morning*

From the reference to the Plain, which I imagine is Salisbury Plain, I surmise that the song is of local origin, with watching the sun rise perhaps referring to a vigil at Stonehenge, such as is still undertaken at Midsummer.

However, just before my time more of the old customs were still being observed. A visitor to Salisbury and Wilton in 1896 met little girls parading the streets with garlands of flowers, fastened to sticks, which they showed to passers-by, who were expected to put something in the collecting-bag. The Wilton garland-bearers sang a little song, concluding with the line 'Please give a penny for the garland'. The Salisbury children did not sing but carried more elaborate garlands.

The custom of making May Day garlands was very widespread. In *The Folklore of the Cotswolds* (1974) Katharine Briggs, quoting late nineteenth-century descriptions, writes:

'The covering of this garland was a day's work, and 30 April was devoted to it in the schools. Some of the boys had walked six or eight miles on the Sunday before to fetch primroses from distant woods, and a great store of flowers, wild and cultivated, was needed to cover the frame. The final topknot was made of crown imperials . . . .

In *The Folklore of Hampshire* (1976) Wendy Boase mentions by name several villages which paraded garlands on May Day but says that 'many years ago nearly every village in Hampshire and the Isle of Wight had its May or Garland Day'. She adds that often the May Queen, crowned with a crown of blossoming hawthorn, went from house to house with the garland-bearers. Her crowning was the climax of the May Day celebrations.

Hampshire and Sussex are two of the counties which preserve a full version of the verse sung by the children who paraded with their garlands. The most common seems to be:

> *The first of May is Garland Day,*
> *So please remember the garland;*
> *We don't come here but once a year,*
> *So please remember the garland.*

An almost identical song is recorded for East Anglia, where, up to the time of the First World War, children used to parade not with garlands but with dolls dressed in all the finery they could concoct. The dolls were carried in a basket or framed in a garlanded hoop and covered with a cloth when a passer-by responded in the affirmative to an invitation to 'see the May Lady'. A gift of a coin or sweets was expected in return.

Dolls decorated with flowers were also carried around some Devonshire villages late in the nineteenth century, the children chanting the verse:

> *We wish you a happy May;*
> *We come to show our May garland,*
> *Because it's the first of May.*
> *Come kiss my face,*
> *And smell my mace,*
> *And give the little children*
> *Something!*

A Devonshire writer of 1874 (Mrs H. P. Whitcombe, in *Bygone Days in Devon and Cornwall*) mentions three places in which garlanded dolls were carried around the streets but says that this was on Oak Apple Day, 29 May. The dolls, she says, were called 'May babies' and were often carried in white boxes. At Bishopsteignton the boys, too, paraded, carrying short poles decorated with flowers, and at Edelesborough the children sang a song of welcome to summer.

John Brand, in *Observations of Popular Antiquities* (1900), describes how he has

'more than once been disturbed early on May morning at Newcastle-on-Tyne by the noise of a song which a woman sung about the streets who has several garlands in her hands, and which she sold to whoever would buy them. It is homely and low . . . .

> *Rise up, maidens, fy for shame!*
> *For I've been four lang miles from hame;*
> *I've been gathering my garlands gay;*
> *Rise up, fair maids, and take in your May.'*

10 Parading the Garland, at Abbotsbury, Dorset, 1935

In Oxford the garlands formerly took the form of crosses, decorated with leaves, bluebells and cuckoo-flowers and carried by small boys, not girls. A similar tradition is recorded for Charlton-on-Otmoor, in Oxfordshire.

Parading with garlands seems in rather earlier times to have been particularly associated with milkmaids. *Chambers' Book of Days* (1854) comments: 'In the course of the morning the eyes of the householders would be greeted by the sight of a milch-cow, all garlanded with flowers, led along by a small group of dairy-women, who, in light and fantastic dresses and with heads wreathed in flowers, would dance around the animal to the sound of a violin or clarinet.'

And Brand (see above) quotes a French writer who describes how

'on the first of May and the five or six days following all the pretty young country girls that serve the town with milk dress themselves up very neatly and borrow abundance of silver plate, whereof they make a pyramid which they adorn with ribands and flowers and carry upon their heads, instead of their common milk-pails. In this equipage, accompanied by some of their fellow milkmaids and a bagpipe or fiddle, they go from door to door, dancing before the houses of their customers, in the midst of boys and girls that follow them in troops, and everybody gives them something.'

Garland-bearing by children and the caperings of milkmaids are evidently among the last, pale survivals of much more full-blooded Maytime celebrations. The dolls and the milkmaids represented the Queen of the May, who once presided over the festivities. *Chambers' Book of Days* describes how 'she was placed in a sort of bower or arbour, near the Maypole, there to sit in pretty state, an object of admiration to the whole village. She herself was half covered with flowers, and her shrine was wholly composed of them.'

The writer thought the office rather a dull one, though he surmised that girls probably enjoy sitting around and looking pretty. But even at that time (1854) he was dealing with a watered-down version of former licentious rites. Chaucer, poet of an earlier age and a man accustomed to call a spade a spade, was aware of what went on in the greenwood on the previous night, when he wrote,

> Hail to the floures, red and white and blewe,
> Which by their vertue maketh our lust newe,

adding that the sight of the flowers and leaves and the singing of the birds 'bringeth into hertes remembraunce and lustie thoughtes full of grete longinge.'

The May Queen is an inevitable feature of all twentieth-century revivals of May Day festivals, for the reason that almost every committee which decides to hold any sort of rural festival today feels that a pretty girl to preside over the event as 'Queen' is essential. Thus we have Carnival Queens, May Queens, Wassail Queens, Dairy Queens, Rally Queens, Harvest Queens and, for aught I know, Shrimp-netting Queens and Electronic Communication Systems Queens. It is therefore difficult to determine whether a Queen gracing modern May Day

11 Little girls by Maypole at Rusholme, Lancashire

12 The May Queen's Float, at Solihull, 1878

celebrations really represents an unbroken tradition from the distant past or whether she is an inspiration that the organisers had last winter, — the latter being the more likely if she happens to be the chairman's daughter or girlfriend.

For all that, a May Queen was an integral part of traditional May Day revels, and in some places there is evidence that observance of the old custom has been more or less continuous. There are three villages in Bedfordshire, for instance — Caldecote, Ickwell and Old Warden — which share a May Queen and have done so for at least 400 years. Girls of 15 years or under from any of the villages are eligible for election. Writing in 1941 Christina Hole says that 'the May Queen has survived in almost every place where May-day celebrations are held' and that 'most villages now have their elected May Queen, and so do the majority of London schools,' but I fancy she may have been misinformed, for in the previous two decades I knew of no such celebrations in any village within 20 or 30 miles of the village in south-eastern Wiltshire which was my home.

Christina Hole adds that in times past a May King shared the honours with the May Queen, but he seems to have been lost sight of long ago, unless he has become confused with Jack o' the Green or the Chimney Sweep or one of the other characters involved in the May Day festivities, of the chief of which we will now take note.

Jack o' the Green, or Jack in the Green, is a figure who appears almost entirely covered with greenery. He is in some districts identified with a chimney sweep,

13 May Day procession, with 'Jack in the Green', outside Balliol College, Oxford, 1886

and in places it seems to have been the prerogative of the local sweeps to choose, dress and parade the Jack. At Amesbury, in Wiltshire, people were alive in the 1930s who could remember the May Day Feast, which was also known there as 'The Sweeps' Holiday'. It was recollected that 'the May Queen danced with the Chimney Sweep'. In *The Folklore of Sussex* (1973) Jacqueline Simpson quotes old Henry Burstow, who was born in 1826, on his memories of May Day in Horsham:

'On this day, too, we had Jacks-in-the Green. The chimney sweeps used to dress up in fancy costumes and in evergreens and flowers, and, accompanied by a fiddler or two, parade and dance all round the town and neighbourhood. There were two sets of Jacks-in-the-Green when I was a boy . . . and considerable rivalry existed between them . . . .'

Wendy Boase, in *The Folklore of Hampshire* (1976), describing May Day celebrations at St Mary Bourne, writes:

'An open space near the church was decorated with a green bower, and here the chimney sweeps gathered for their special celebrations. They appeared on May Day, elaborately dressed and carrying the tools of their trade, to dance around the ''Jack-in-the-Green''. This strange figure, a man dressed as a tree, symbolised spring itself and was adopted by the sweeps as their own ''walking bower''. Clattering their brushes and shovels against each other, the sweeps cavorted round Jack-in-the-Green, while boys blew their May-horns of twisted willow bark.'

A similar custom was observed at Hurstbourne Priors, in the same county. And in *Cambridgeshire Customs and Folklore* (1969) Enid Porter states:

'May Day was the traditional holiday for chimney sweeps who, until last century, wearing their top-hats, took an important part in old May Day festivities. A procession of dancers, headed by *Jack in the Green,* the local sweep, who walked in a framework of boughs, made their way through the village (Melbourn) to the Maypole.'

In Devonshire Mrs A. Bray, writing of Tavistock in 1832, says:

'We now generally see only the verdant pyramid crowned with flowers. This pyramid joins the procession and sometimes even the dances; it receives its motion from having concealed within it a good stout fellow; strong and tall enough to perform his part for the day. Jack-in-the-Bush is his name; and he has existed (so I am told) as long as the Maypole itself.'

Another frequent character in May Day drama was Robin Hood, appropriately for a greenwood festival. In one version of the Helston May Song occurs the verse:

> *Robin Hood and Little John, they both are gone to fair-O,*
> *And we will to the merry greenwood to see what they do there-O,*
> *And for to chase-O, to chase the buck and doe.*
> *Hal-an-Tow, jolly rumble-O*
> *And for to fetch the Summer Home, the Summer and the May-O,*
> *For summer is a-come-O, and Winter is a-gone-O.*

It evidently belongs to a sort of mumming-play, in which Robin Hood was a principal character. Such plays were apparently performed widely in the midlands until the time of the Commonwealth. Robin seems to have been identical with the May King, and Maid Marian, his consort, with the May Queen.

Associated with the plays and with the festivities in general were several strange beasts or dragons, a number of which survive in different forms, of which the Hobby Horse is the commonest.

One of the best known of English hobby horses is the Padstow Oss, which Tony Deane and Tony Shaw, in *The Folklore of Cornwall* (1975), describe as

'a grotesque and frightening creature portrayed by a man with a bulbous black cape, topped by a ferocious mask. There are, in fact, two hobby horses, as well as the ''Boys' Osses'' or ''Colts''. Today the Blue Ribbon Oss appears first ...it is not until an hour later, when the Old (Red Ribbon) Oss dances from its traditional stable . . . that the atmosphere in Padstow becomes truly electric. Each horse is accompanied by its team of Mayers, all dressed in white shirts and trousers, sailors' caps and either red or blue sashes denoting their allegiance to a particular horse, and each team is led by a master of ceremonies, wearing a morning suit and top-hat. A "teaser" prances before each horse, brandishing a decorated club; once he, too, was masked, but now goes bare-faced . . . .'

There are several interesting subsidiary features of the ceremony. The Oss is black and, in an old version, he used to select a victim to be smeared with soot. The tradition suggests a link with the May Day chimney sweeps. The Oss also used to visit a pool in the neighbourhood — Treator Pool — where he splashed the spectators with water for luck. And there is a belief among Padstow people that any girl touched by the Oss will have a baby within the year. It may be significant that at the end of his parade the Oss dies but is later resurrected and joins in the feasting.

Minehead, on the Exmoor coast, also has a Hobby Horse which parades on May Day. The Minehead event is, in fact, a three-day festival, starting on 30 April, which is the 'Warning Eve' and continuing through 1 and 2 May. R.W. Patten, in *Exmoor Custom and Song* (1974), gives this description of the Horse:

'The animal is constructed of a wooden frame, 7 to 8 feet long, carried on the shoulders of a man whose body is mostly concealed by houselling made of

14 Minehead Hobby Horse

sacking, decorated with brightly coloured circles and bearing the title
SAILORS HORSE The head is in the centre of the framework, surmounted by a
tall conical and be-ribboned cap perched over a grotesque mask which hides the
man's face. A profusion of multi-coloured ribbons covers the whole of the
upper part of the framework, and a long tail of rope trails behind. If it were
not for the tail, the whole contraption would resemble not so much a horse as a
ship, and this perhaps is a key to the riddle.'

The Minehead Horse, having put in a brief appearance on Warning Eve, spends
May Day parading around town and in the evening goes to the neighbouring little
town of Dunster, where it is entertained by the lord of the manor, capers around
the market place and then returns to Minehead. On the following day it makes the
rounds of Minehead, in a ceremony which is obviously allied to beating the
bounds, for in old times any victim the Horse caught had the option of paying a
fine or being beaten on the bottom, ten times, with an old boot. This custom is
now observed at one point only in Minehead. In those days the Horse was
provided with a pair of snappers, with which it could grab a spectator, but these
have now been abolished. The Horse now prances around and bows to onlookers
when soliciting baksheesh. In earlier times, too, the Minehead Horse was preceded
by an attendant, as the Padstow Oss still is. This character, known as a gulliver,
carried a club and wore a mask and a ribboned costume.
   Minehead now has two Horses, the second being the Town Horse, who seems to
have originated at a later date and who contents itself with a shorter parade.
   Mr Patten's suggestion that the similarity of the Horse to a ship might hold a
clue to its meaning is interesting, for there are several instances of May Day
celebrations in the West Country featuring decorated ships. One Padstow legend
ascribes the May Day festivities to rejoicing over the defeat of a shipload of French
invaders during the Napoleonic wars, while another Minehead story maintains that
the parade of the Hobby Horse commemorates a victory over the Danes, who also
came by ship. On the other hand, hobby horses are to be found in many parts of
the country, often associated with other festivals than May Day. Some examples
are noted later. And a Cornish tradition declares that horseshoes, hanging on
house walls to ward off witches, have to be taken down and turned on May Day,
without touching the ground. The weird masks worn by the horses are, in some
respects, reminiscent of the Dorset 'Ooser' (see page 21), though this fearsome
animal now appears at Christmas-time and seems to resemble a bull rather than a
horse.
   Combe Martin, in North Devon, also had a hobby horse once, and in the 1830s
Mrs Bray heard vague recollections of one at Tavistock. In Wiltshire the Hobby
Horse kept in the museum at Salisbury joins street processions on special
occasions, such as coronations and jubilees, but was formerly associated with
particular festivals, notably Midsummer (St John's Night), 16 July (St Osmund's
Night — St Osmund being a local saint), 1 August (St Peter's Night) and May
Day.

In fact, the Hobby Horse was a character in the ancient folk drama which now survives chiefly as mumming plays, now usually held to be traditional at Christmas but formerly performed at festivals right around the year. He was closely associated with Morris dancers.

Two even more essential features than the hobby horse of the May Day celebrations were the maypole and the Morris dancers. The Morris dance is supposed by some to derive its name from 'Moorish', on the assumption that it was introduced to England from some outlandish place such as the land of the Moors, but the dance itself has apparently been little changed since the fifteenth century and was probably performed in many parts of the country long before that. In recent years a strong revival of interest in Morris dancing has occurred, some companies resurrecting an ancient local tradition while others have been formed without the benefit of local antecedents.

The version of the Morris dance performed in most of midland and southern England is for six men who perform intricate movements, in which they make use of short staves, handkerchiefs and hand-clapping. They wear flower-decked hats, or in some instances caps, white shirts and knee-breeches, much be-ribboned, and cross-gartered hose. Small bells are often attached to their costumes. In Lancashire versions of the dance the dancers wore clogs. The accompanying music is usually played on an accordion or concertina, and memory indicates that these instruments were traditional. Edith Olivier, collecting items of Wiltshire folklore

15 Morris Dancers drinking the King's health, Stratford-on-Avon, 1904

in the 1920s and 1930s, noted that for an old May Day dance at the Cross Stones in Durrington, not far from Stonehenge, the accompaniment was provided by concertinas and whistle-pipes. The May Day celebrations at Padstow have their attendant bands of 'accordions, melodeons and drums'. An early record from the Cotswolds refers to a 'whistle about a foot long, together with a small flat drum, hung on the performer's finger and beaten with a short drumstick'. Nowhere have the Morris dance traditions been better preserved than in the Cotswolds. Many of the old tunes and songs have been collected, and booklets have been published by modern Morris Men teams. A summary of the mass of information available is found in Katharine Briggs' *The Folklore of the Cotswolds,* 1974.

Morris dancers traditionally performed around the maypole, a former feature of almost every English village green, as well as of city streets and churchyards. Sometimes the pole stayed in position until it decayed, when it was replaced by a new one; more often it was taken down after the annual celebrations and stored until the next year; and in some instances a new one was cut each year.

In many places the conventional tree for a maypole was the hawthorn, or may, but in others there seems to have been no general rule. John Brand, discussing maypoles in his *Observations on Popular Antiquities* (1900), incidentally mentions oak, birch and elm as being traditional in various localities. Sometimes the maypoles were painted, often with spiralling stripes of bright colours, and some of them, particularly in towns, were elaborately decorated.

Many old-time writers refer to the great height of some of the poles. John Stow in his *Survey of London* (1598) mentions the maypole which was erected every year 'in the midst of the street before the south door of the said church (St Andrew's Undershaft); which shaft, when it was set on end and fixed in the ground, was higher than the church steeple'. *Chambers' Book of Days* (1854) describes the great maypole that was erected in The Strand in the first year after the Restoration, 1661. He refers to it as a cedar and says it was 134 feet high. *Folklore, Myths and Legends of Britain* (1973) notes that probably the oldest and tallest maypole in England is at Barwick in Elmet, Yorkshire. It is taken down for re-painting and re-decoration once every three years.

Evidently it was a practice in many places to increase the height of the pole by erecting it on an elevation or by making an artificial hillock for the purpose. *Chambers' Book of Days* cites the example of the maypole at Welford, in Warwickshire, about five miles from Stratford-on-Avon: 'It is of great height and is planted in the centre of a raised mound, to which there is an ascent by three stone steps; on this mound the dancers probably performed their gyrations.' In her account of the former May Day festivities at Durrington, on Salisbury Plain, Edith Olivier notes that 'the men went to the downs and got a may-bush and then to the Nag's Head Inn for the May-pole. They tied the bush to the top of the May-pole and chained the pole to the top of the Cross Stones'. At Horncastle, Lincolnshire, it was held to be essential that the May Day procession should start from a top of a hill, known as May Bank, on the opposite side of the town to the maypole.

Cornwall has an interesting tradition of maypole raiding. Gangs of young men would attempt to steal the maypole of a neighbouring village, an expedition which often culminated in a boisterous battle. To protect their poles, the villagers used to mount guard on the nights before and after May Day. Tony Deane and Tony Shaw in *The Folklore of Cornwall* (1975) state that the custom is still observed in the village of Lanreath. Enemy agents from the neighbouring villages try to make the guards fall asleep by offering them too much liquor, while the Lanreath contingent counter by letting down the tyres of scouting enemy vehicles. In this instance the maypole is not kept for use in the following year but is chopped up for making skittles.

The May Day celebrations at Durrington (Wiltshire) referred to above were observed not on the present 1 May but on Old May Day, which corresponds to the present 13 May. The change of calendar in 1752 presented a number of problems to villagers bent on keeping up the old customs. Although the English weather is never reliable, there is a better chance of favourable conditions for outdoor activities on 13 May than on 1 May. At least the weather should be a little warmer. This was one of the chief reasons for the dispersal of traditional May Day customs to other points of the calendar. The period of the Commonwealth, dominated by the pleasure-hating Puritans, also imposed an hiatus from which some of the old country customs never properly recovered. The Puritans reserved a particular hatred for the May Day festivities, and the popular reaction at the time of the Restoration was naturally focused on the new pleasure-loving monarch, Charles II, who became especially associated with Oak Apple Day, 29 May. Accordingly, in

16 Morris Dancers at Knutsford

many places the revived May Day institutions were switched to Oak Apple Day. In others, Whitsuntide (which is more likely to occur around 13 May than 1 May) inherited the May Day traditions. The similarity between the spring-tide customs now upheld on various dates throughout the month of May demonstrates their common origin but also serves to remind us that they were evolved to celebrate the arrival of spring and so referred to a season rather than to an unalterable date.

For instance, the now well-known Furry Dance of Helston, in Cornwall, is an obvious May festival, though its date is now the nearest Saturday to 8 May. Furry Dance and Floral Dance — the dance performed during the celebrations to a tune taught in schools throughout England — are synonymous; 'Furry' is the word used locally. The dance continues through the streets all day long and attracts crowds of sightseers. The dancers wear their best clothes and wear or carry bunches of spring flowers, lilies of the valley being a favourite. When they find a street door open they dance through the house, to bring good luck to the residents.

In recent years a former feature of the festival, long defunct, has been revived. Called the Hal-an-Tow, it is evidently a form of Maytime mumming play, with Robin Hood, Little John, St George and someone called Aunt Mary Moses, who seems to correspond to Maid Marian, as the chief characters. The tune to which the Hal-an-Tow song is sung is quite different from the one played for the dance.

Christina Hole (*English Custom and Usage,* 1941) comments that, although the inhabitants of Helston do not spend the night of 7 May 'in the open, as their ancestors did, the green branches are brought in early in the morning, and every house is decorated with them'. Another place where this ancient tradition is meticulously followed is Wishford, in Wiltshire, though here the date is now fixed as 29 May, Oak Apple Day. It has, however, little or nothing to do with celebrating the Restoration of Charles II, which is the ostensible purpose of Oak Apple Day, for there is documentary evidence that it was an 'Ancient Custom' as far back as the reign of Henry VIII. It was then held on Whit Tuesday.

The celebrations, in which I have quite often taken part, start at about 2.30 a.m., when the village children and teenagers parade around the village, making a terrific hullabaloo and banging at doors until each householder looks out and promises to be up in the greenwood by first light. The greenwood in this case is the Forest of Grovely, a large area of mostly deciduous woodland extending along the crest of a hill a mile or so away. Every household has to send a representative to cut green boughs and carry them down the hill to decorate the house. Prizes are offered for the best decorations, and also for the oak-tree branch bearing the greatest number of oak apples (the work of a little gall-fly, *Biorrhiza terminalis*). A party of strong men drag along a great oak bough and hoist it to the tower of St Giles' Church.

About mid-morning a party of Wishford villagers, in early Victorian costumes, board a coach for the journey to Salisbury. There they march into the Cathedral and present green oak boughs to the Dean before the high altar. This done, their leader raises the traditional shout, 'Grovely! Grovely! Grovely! and all Grovely!' Emerging from the Cathedral by way of the great west door, they form a circle on

17 Helston Furry Dance, the dancers dancing in and out of the houses

the lawn, where six or eight of them perform the dance belonging to the occasion before returning home.

Until a hundred or so years ago the performance was followed by a fair, with stalls, sideshows and sports, in the Cathedral churchyard. This has now been transferred back to Wishford. On their annual excursion to the Cathedral, too, the villagers had to pay a tribute of 'pentecostals' or 'smoke farthings'. Even earlier, they had to provide the forest ranger with 'one white Loaf and one Gallon of Beer and A Pair of Gloves or twelvepence in money', as a reward for presenting them with half a fat buck from the forest. If he failed to fulfil his side of the bargain, they had the right to enter the woods and kill a buck for themselves.

All this is supposed to establish the villagers' rights in the forest, rights which one of the Earls of Pembroke (local landlords) tried unsuccessfully to suppress two centuries or so ago. But that is evidently a later accretion to age-old spring-time festivities connected with the greenwood. The custom of bringing green boughs home in triumph must once have been widespread, for in the neighbouring county of Hampshire Wendy Boase has been able to collect a number of examples.

At Newport, in the Isle of Wight,

'on the Sunday after May Day the people rose before dawn to gather boughs of hawthorn and other trees. Anyone who did not do this was fined a gallon of wine and a goose. The return from the woods to the town resembled a triumphal procession, the people leading with green boughs and the forest keepers, the town bailiffs, the minstrels, morris dancers and town sergeants following. Later in the morning the greenery was hung over the doors and round the windows of every house in Newport, and the bailiffs were presented with small green boughs by the keepers of the forest in recognition of their authority . . . .'

Many places in mainland Hampshire had similar celebrations. In *It Happened in Hampshire,* a Women's Institute collection published in 1937, 14 villages which kept up May Day in this or similar ways are mentioned by name, and the compilers comment, 'Nearly every village had its May Day.' Delving back deep into history, we find Chaucer in *The Court of Love* (though some have claimed that this is not his work) commenting, 'Forth goeth all the court, both most and least, to fetch the flowers fresh' early on May Day morning. The 'court' evidently meant the royal household, for in the reign of Henry VIII the king and queen went out from Greenwich to meet the chief dignitaries of the City of London when they went out into Kent, a-Maying. The boys of Eton school carried on the old customs by rising at four in the morning to gather green branches for decorating the school windows.

In some of the eastern counties it seems that a certain symbolism governed the decorations. Writes W. K. Clay, in his *History of Waterbeach* (Cambridgeshire), 1895:

'The young woman who had been foremost in the dance and whose amiable manners had entitled her to our esteem had a large branch or tree of whitethorn planted by her cottage door; the girl of loose manners had a blackthorn planted by hers; the slattern had an elder tree planted by hers; and the scold a bunch of nettles tied to the latch of her cottage door.'

Having completed their rounds, the lads collected a garland, which they had previously prepared, and suspended it over the village street, by cords attached to chimneys on either side. All had to be done before sunrise. Christina Hole *(English Custom and Usage,* 1941) mentions the same custom for Hertfordshire, while in Cheshire the plants attached to each house had names rhyming with some notable characteristic of the occupants.

May Day celebrations, with the emphasis on the greenwood, are traditional all over Europe. They were enjoyed, for several days after 28 April, by the Romans as the Festival of Floralia. Roman festivals tended to deteriorate into orgies, the Saturnalia, which occurred around Christmas-time, having become notorious on that account. An echo of the former lawless associations of May Day may be detected in Mischief Night, 30 April, at Burnley (Lancashire), where, according to Christina Hole, 'shopkeepers' signs were changed, gates were taken off their hinges and hidden, and all sorts of practical jokes were played, until the custom . . . was finally stopped by the police'. In Wiltshire when I was a boy in the 1920s we regarded 5 November in much the same light and thought that we were immune from interference by the law.

In the British Isles, however, 1 May had a further significance in that it was one of the quarter days of the old pagan, pastoral calendar. It was the Celtic Beltane, or Beallteinn, a word which according to some authorities means 'a goodly fire', and some of the customs associated with May Day celebrations are concerned with fire. Margaret Killip, in *The Folklore of the Isle of Man* (1975), notes:

'Flowers and fire were the chief features of the ritual of Beltain, for the people set fire to the gorse on the hills and on the field hedges "to burn out the witches", and the smoke blew over the fields and purified them, and they drove their cattle between the fires. When the gorse fires were all blazing and the hedges alight, the hillside seemed to be crisscrossed with "walls of fire", and to add further terror to the scene, *dollans,* skin drums, were beaten and horns blown all through the night "to drive away the bad spirits". When all these rites had been observed, and no precaution omitted, "then the fields were ready to put the cattle on the grass".'

The fires were held to be therapeutic, cattle being driven between or through them as a precaution against murrain. And in Shetland men and boys had to jump through the bonfires kindled for the Beltane feast. The fires were kept burning for three days and nights, and respects were paid to the rising sun each morning. In mainland Scotland in the eighteenth century a man was chosen by lot to be the 'Beltane carle'. He had the duty of jumping through a Beltane fire three times. There seem here to be faint reminiscences of former human sacrifices, no doubt performed to help the fertility of the soil and so produce a good harvest. It

18 Maypole Dancing at
Kingkerswell in Devon,
c.1900

is recorded that when Bishop Hugh Latimer was burnt at the stake in October
1555, a spectator was heard to remark that it was a pity that the event could not
have been staged earlier in the season, when it could have saved the crops!

At Holne, on the fringe of Dartmoor, a ram was traditionally slaughtered on
this day. After it had been run down after a gruelling chase over the moor it was
fastened to a granite post, six or seven feet high, in the middle of a field and
slaughtered. It was then roasted whole, unskinned, and at midday was sliced up
and given to the crowd. Young men would struggle for a slice to present to their
girls. The ram had to be killed so that the blood from the wound in its throat
flowed over the base of the stone and the ground around it.

At Kingsteignton, in the same district, a ram is killed, roasted and distributed
to the crowd of merry-makers, who have assembled for a traditional festival.

Coupled with these ancient pagan associations was the fact that fertility, and
the sexual act involved, was very much in people's minds at this season. The
maypole itself is considered by some to represent the human phallus. Knowing
well what went on in the woods on the night before May Day, it is no wonder that
the austere Puritans, equating sin with sexual licence, thundered against the May
Day customs. Said one, Thomas Hall (Funebriae Florae, 1660): 'If Moses were
angry when he saw the people dance about a golden calf, well may we be angry to
see people dancing the morrice about a post in honour of a whore . . . .'

The whore was Maid Marian, or the Queen of the May, regarded by the Puritans as the Scarlet Woman, the Whore of Babylon, referred to in *The Book of Revelation*. A very different identification from the modern one of a mediaeval girl taking to the greenwood with her outlawed lover.

Long before the Puritan era the early Christian fathers, realising the futility of trying to force their new converts to abandon all of their former beliefs and customs, adopted the policy of taking over the ancient pagan festivals and transforming them into Christian ones. They succeeded with Christmas, Easter, All Saints' Day and others, but they could never do much with May Day.

*   *   *

A few May Day customs which seem to have little or nothing to do with the main celebrations remain to be noticed.

It is said, in many parts of the country, that May kittens do not make good cats and should be drowned. In Orkney and Shetland the belief applies particularly to kittens born 'between the Beltanes', which is between 1 and 8 May but is extended to other animals as well. Chickens hatched from eggs set under hens between those dates will also never thrive. In some districts a May Day baby is held to be unlucky.

In Orkney, too, it was a custom for young people to climb to the hill-tops on May Day morning to bathe their faces in May dew. A similar belief was current in Cornwall, where May dew, as well as being a cosmetic, was regarded as of great value in curing neck ailments, provided it was collected from the grave of a newly-buried corpse. Another version says that the dew must be gathered by going before dawn on May Day to the grave of the last young man to be buried in the churchyard. The sufferer must pass his hand over the surface of the grave, from head to foot, three times, immediately transferring the dew to the affected part. In Somerset May dew was even effective against freckles.

Margaret Killip, in *The Folklore of the Isle of Man* (1975), speaks of the joy with which the return of spring was greeted. It was, she says,

'celebrated with a ritual gathering and strewing of the first plants and flowers of the season, symbols of the rebirth of life and power in all growing things. On the Eve of May Day green branches and yellow flowers were gathered and spread around the doors and windows of dwelling houses and cattle sheds; branches of *tramman* (elder) were hung up, and the twigs of mountain ash were made into crosses and placed over doorways and hidden in the long hair of the tails of cattle to protect them from harm.'

Yellow flowers were apparently the most effective against witchcraft, and especially the primrose and the marsh marigold, the latter being known as 'the herb of Beltain'.

Mountain ash and bay are also reckoned potent against witches in Somerset, and certain herbs, kept dried during the winter, had to be disposed of by May Day, by ritual burning. They included hemlock, sloe, rue and rosemary. In

Cambridgeshire May Day was the best day for gathering dandelions for making wine; and peat fires were allowed to go out on the hearth.

In the remoter parts of Britain, where Celtic influence is strong, May Day customs associated with standing stones, considered magical and sacred, survived until the nineteenth century and may, indeed, still do so. It was considered unlucky by the inhabitants of the neighbourhood not to visit the well-known standing stones of Callanish, on the Isle of Skye, on May Day. At Perranarworthal, in Cornwall, a trilithon known as the Cornish Pebble was said to cure sufferers from rheumatism and sciatica if, during early May, they would crawl around it and then squeeze through between the two supporting stones. In Perthshire one could secure a wish by visiting a well at Tullybelton, in Strathtay, on the morning of 1 May, drinking the water and then walking round the well nine times clockwise, followed by a similar circumambulation of standing stones nearby.

Contradictory to all the traditions concerning the new and exuberant life of early May is one, recorded by Enid Porter in *Cambridgeshire Customs and Folklore* (1969), to the effect that, in the Fens around Ely and Littleport, 'anyone who was out early on May Day morning would see the ghosts of all those who had been drowned in the Fen rivers and dykes'. Superstitious Fenmen kept their boats tied up that morning. The belief would seem to be connected with the ancient festival which the Romans called Lemuralia, the Feast of the Dead, held on 9 May. There may also be a connection with the strange superstition that it is unlucky to marry in May.

Finally, May sees the beginning of the mackerel season for fishermen, and Sussex fishermen used to regard it as especially lucky if the first mackerel came in on 1 May. Brighton fishermen held a feast, 'Bendin'-In', on the beach to celebrate it.

May has inspired the usual crop of agricultural proverbs, some of them contradictory. 'Wet May; long hay' makes good sense, but I am not so sure about

> *Cold May and windy,*
> *Barn filleth up finely.*

It apparently rests on the assumption that cool and windy weather in May suits corn crops, which, I think, is seldom confirmed by events.

> *Shear your sheep in May*
> *And you'll shear them all away*

is sound advice. Shearing is undertaken not only to take the wool clip but also to help protect the sheep from attacks by flies, which lay their eggs in the wool. There is therefore an incentive to shear early, before flies become numerous, but it is mistaken enterprise if the sheep take chill in cold, wet weather immediately afterwards; and in May we are still in the danger zone for that sort of weather.

> *Who sows in May*
> *Gets little that way*

is a proverb relating to oats. Apart from the fact that May is a late date for sowing any sort of cereals, spring-sown oats are very vulnerable to attacks by the frit-fly, at least in southern England, and May is the month when the frit-fly is about. The oats should be past the four-leaf stage by then, to avoid trouble.

A cottagers' proverb, formerly well known, relates to bees:

A swarm of bees in May
Is worth a load of hay.
A swarm of bees in June
Is worth a silver spoon.
A swarm of bees in July
Isn't worth a fly.

Before beekeepers resorted to the artificial feeding of bees in winter, the bees needed as long a summer as possible to store enough honey to last them through the dark months. That is, those hives which were earmarked for survival, but, of course, it was the custom to destroy the swarms from which honey was collected in autumn, and with these, too, the longer the gathering season the larger the honey store. But a swarm of bees in May is comparatively rare. Its rarity value could indeed perhaps be compared to that of a load of hay.

CHAPTER 6

Rogationtide, Ascensiontide & Whitsuntide

AS TOUCHED upon in the previous chapter, many of the May Day festivities have become dispersed to other dates throughout May, some even in April and June. This has happened largely through Puritan influence in the middle decades of the seventeenth century, which caused an hiatus in their celebration during the period of the Commonwealth. When after the Restoration in 1660 the old customs were revived, their attachment to certain traditional dates was less adhesive than before, and alterations were made to suit local convenience.

In many instances May Day customs seem to have slipped back to Easter; in many others they were moved to Oak Apple Day, 29 May. The Wishford Oak Apple Day celebrations, already described (see pages 70-72), are a notable example. In the England of the 1660s Oak Apple Day was, of course, extremely popular. The story of Charles II hiding from his pursuers in the Boscobel Oak caught public imagination. The date when he had this adventure was not 29 May but 4 September, but with 29 May marking the date of his Restoration to the throne the opportunity to merge it with the age-old May celebrations concerned with the greenwood in general and the oak in particular was too good to miss.

Some of the May Day festivities were moved more than once. Barwick-in-Elmet, West Yorkshire, has an 80-foot maypole which is taken down for repainting every three years on Easter Monday. It is re-erected on Whit Tuesday, with a programme of typical May Day junketings. Beyond much doubt, here were May Day revels which swung first to one side of the traditional date, then to the other. At Uplyme, east Devon, maypole dancing is also held on Whit Tuesday, since its merging, at some time in the nineteenth century, with the local Club Fete. Before that the traditional date was Good Friday; and before that, probably May Day.

Before proceeding with an examination of some of the customs which cluster around this congested season, it may be as well to remind ourselves of the salient points in the Church calendar. Forty days after Easter comes Ascension Day, or Holy Thursday. Ten days after Ascension Day, Whitsuntide. The three days prior to Ascension Day are known as Rogationtide, and the Sunday before them is Rogation Sunday. The next Sunday after Whit Sunday is Trinity Sunday. The Thursday after Trinity Sunday is Corpus Christi, a festival kept by the Roman Catholic but not by Protestant churches.

It is also worth remembering why May should be such a busy month for merry-making and rural festivals. The explanation is that not only is May one of the pleasantest and most inspiring months of the year but, in the agricultural calendar, one of the slackest. By the beginning of May, all crops should have been sown. Cows and sheep are grazing in vividly green pastures and need little attention. The lambs are growing but are not yet big enough for slaughter, and the shearing season does not normally begin till June. Modern gardeners, devoting themselves to exotic crops of which our ancestors knew nothing, find plenty of work to do in May, but for old-time farmers and peasants the month was as near as they could get to a summer holiday season. What we now regard as the summer holiday period, from mid-July to mid-September, was for them the busiest season of the year — the time of harvest. Even today this apparent reversal of the accepted order still applies to agriculturists. Few if any farmers could think of taking a holiday between early July and late September, and May is the month in which they can most easily get away from the farm.

One of the features of life in great numbers of nineteenth-century English villages was the Village Club. In origin it was a local insurance society against sickness. The headquarters were usually the village inn. Members paid weekly dues and were entitled to draw sick pay when ill until the money ran out. Few seem to have attempted to build up a permanent fund. Most were 'slate clubs', so-called because the accounts were kept on a slate, which was wiped clean at the end of each year. Any credit balance was used to provide the beer and victuals at the annual Club Festival.

The choice of Whitsuntide for most Club Festivals was doubtless influenced by the factors mentioned above. Men could afford to take a day off from farm work. There was also a tradition of Whitsuntide feasts, or Whitsun Ales, which we shall consider shortly, and it is likely that many clubs simply took over the old customs.

In the Wiltshire village where I was a boy in the 1920s elderly men could still remember the Whitsuntide Club feasts, which apparently died out in the 1880s. It seems that there was nothing outstanding in the programme. My father remembered that one old man set up a shooting gallery and rewarded anyone who hit the target with a handful of hazel-nuts, which he himself had collected in the woods in the previous autumn. There were dancing, some sports and a few stalls, but the main ingredient for a jolly day was beer, consumed in such quantities that abstemious wives and the few teetotal men had their work cut out, carrying the others home at bedtime.

In an era when teetotalism was becoming an important factor in village life, these carousals met with increasing opposition, particularly from Nonconformists, who deliberately organised their Sunday School anniversaries to clash with the older events. When the clubs were eventually superseded by national insurance companies, the Sunday Schools were left masters of the field. In some districts, declining in numbers, they still hold their anniversary services and festivals on Whit Sunday, though the substitution of Spring Bank Holiday for the Whitsuntide holiday has caused confusion and the severance of a few more links with the past.

The predecessor of the Club Feast was the Whitsun Ale. John Aubrey, the Wiltshire antiquary, writing before the period of the Commonwealth when the old customs still prevailed, places them in their context:

'There were no rates for the poor in my Grandfather's days; for Kingstone St Michael the Church Ale at Whitsuntide did the business. In every parish is (or was) a church house, to which belonged spits, crocks, etc., utensils for dressing provisions. Here the housekeepers met and were merry, and gave their charity. The young people were there, too, and had dancing, bowling, shooting at butts, etc., the ancients sitting gravely by and looking on. All things were civil, and without scandal.'

One can surmise that these Ales were instituted after the Reformation, to provide some sort of substitute for the charity formerly dispensed by the suppressed religious houses. Although Whitsun was the date chosen for them in some places, in others they were held at Christmas, Michaelmas or at some other convenient time; there was no general rule. An Ale, called the Clerk's Ale because it was supplied by the parish clerk, was still being held on Easter Tuesday as late as 1854 at Chisledon, near Swindon. In this instance, those who attended each brought a present for the clerk, who presumably used the donations to pay the expenses before setting aside the balance for charity. Or perhaps for some other purpose, because some records imply that the proceeds were devoted to the repair of the parish church.

Francis Douce, writing early in the nineteenth century, provides details of how a Whitsun Ale was conducted at that time:

'Two persons are chosen, previously to the meeting, to be lord and lady of the ale, who dress as suitably as they can to the characters they assume. A large, empty barn or some such building is provided for the lord's all and fitted up with seats to accommodate the company. Here they assemble to dance and regale in the best manner their circumstances and the place will afford; and each fellow treats his girl with a riband or favour. The lord and lady honour the hall with their presence, attended by the steward, sword-bearer, purse-bearer and mace-bearer, with their several badges or ensigns of office. They have likewise a train-bearer or page, and a fool or jester, dressed in a parti-coloured jacket, whose ribaldry and gesticulation contribute not a little to the entertainment of some part of the company. The lord's music, consisting of a pipe and tabor, is employed to conduct the dance.'

Richard Carew, writing of Cornwall in the reign of Queen Elizabeth, depicts the Whitsun Ale as a kind of faith feast, to which each contributed according to his means. They met, he says, at the church house 'and there merrily feed on their owne victuals'. The Ales were there organised by the churchwardens, who in due course presented the accounts to the parishoners, the money being used 'to defray any extraordinary charges arising in the parish or imposed on them for the good of the country or the prince's service'. He adds that such impositions were not usually very burdensome, for normally 'somewhat stil remayneth to cover the purse's bottom'.

The sort of festival thus described, conveniently staged in the carefree month of May (or early June), naturally attracted a gallimaufry of local customs thought worth perpetuating. So, in connection with Whitsun feasts and ales, we find references to mumming plays, morris dancers, maypoles, mystery plays and a host of other activities that are also associated with other seasons. Our ancestors evidently considered that one couldn't have too much of a good thing.

A Whitsuntide celebration of undoubted antiquity was the Whit Hunt which took place in Wychwood Forest on Whit Monday, Witney and the neighbouring villages participating. The villagers all assembled at dawn and made a rendezvous at Hailey, from whence they proceeded to hunt. They were allowed three deer, one for each of the villages of Witney, Crawley and Hailey. The man first on the scene when each of the deer was pulled down claimed the head and antlers. The carcases were taken off for the feast, and the skin was cut up and distributed to the hunters.

For the rest of the week celebrations were held in a big barn at Ducklington and around a maypole erected outside it. A feast, called the 'Youth Ale', was held in the barn on the Monday for the returning hunters, but the main feast occurred on the Saturday, when the slain deer were cooked and eaten. Morris dancers were much to the fore all the week, staging expeditions to the various villages and bringing back more recruits for the merry-making in the barn. These celebrations were continued until 1847.

Burford, in the same county, once had a similar custom, which was, however, commuted as early as 1593 to a gift of three deer to the town. These were presented to a boy and girl elected by the town, in the manner described above, to be the Lord and Lady of Whitsun. The gift of deer was continued till 1854, when it was commuted to a cash payment. Another feature of the Whitsun festivities at Burford was a procession in which the effigies of a giant and a dragon were carried. Cirencester also had a Whitsun festival, complete with Lord and Lady, dancers, musicians and a procession.

Kingsteignton, in Devon, held a ram-roasting feast on Whit Tuesday, a custom which was revived, after a long hiatus, in 1885. Its origin was explained locally by the legend that at some distant, forgotten date the village had been short of water and that when intercession was made to the gods a new stream appeared and brought a torrent of water through the parish. The ram lamb was a thanksgiving sacrifice. It had to be roasted on the bed of the stream, which had thus to be diverted a few days before the feast. Maypole dancing is still held at Kingsteignton, I believe, on Whit Monday (or rather, now on Spring Bank Holiday).

A writer in the *Transactions of the Devonshire Association* in 1896 listed 24 places in north Devon alone which still held festivals on Whit Monday, commenting that even this was considerably fewer than 60 years earlier. Her description of the sort of thing that went on includes features which must have been common all over England, though some, such as wrestling (at least in the local style), belonged peculiarly to Devon:

> 'On the morning of the revel hats gaudily trimmed with ribbons were hung up in conspicuous places and were sometimes worn in church as an advertisement that wrestling would take place. Trees were fixed on either side of the door of a house to show that it was a bush house, privileged to sell ale during the revel without being licensed. Standings were erected on the village green, where sweets and gingerbread were sold on the Sunday, and wares of all kinds on the Monday. All classes joined in the games and sports, wrestling, skittles, boxing, running, cock-fighting, climbing the greased pole, football, dancing and cock-shying. Women ran for gowns, legs of mutton and other prizes; men wrestled for hats and silver spoons; boys climbed a greased pole on which was mounted the prize; and young men gave their young women fairings, usually packets of sweets made of almonds, sugar and spice, or gingerbread nuts, or Spanish nuts.'

Costessey, near Norwich, used to have a Mock Mayor, elected on May Day and installed in office, with much ceremony, on Whit Tuesday. The Mayor and his predecessor headed a procession which marched to breakfast at the Falcon Inn early that morning. Characters in the procession included a wickerwork and canvas dragon named Snap, a Dick Fool on a hobby horse and a jester with a bladder on a stick, — those common features of many mediaeval processions. There were also children on white ponies. When, after breakfast, the procession re-formed and went to Costessey Hall for the inauguration ceremony, three of the children, taking the parts of Shepherd, Shepherdess and Orator, presented a playlet in which they recited verses of welcome. The verses have been preserved by Enid Porter in *The Folklore of East Anglia,* but appear to be of no great antiquity, probably early nineteenth- or late eighteenth-century.

Necton and Yarmouth, both in Norfolk, also had Whitsun festivals featuring mock mayors, while Rye, in Sussex, has a ceremony, in late May, in which the real mayor and his councillors scatter hot pennies in the street, for children to scramble for. The Costessey celebrations lasted until 1895.

The Dunmow Flitch trial is a Whit Monday occasion. Staged at Great Dunmow, in Essex, the flitch (a side of bacon) is offered to married couples who can prove that they have never quarrelled or wished themselves single again. Originally held at Little Dunmow, the custom is mentioned by Chaucer in the fourteenth century and is said to have been instituted a hundred years earlier by one Robert Fitzwalter. The

jury used to be the Prior and villagers of Little Dunmow; now it comprises six bachelors and six spinsters. Until the beginning of the eighteenth century only the husband was required to testify, but now, of course, both husband and wife appear and are subjected to a barrage of searching and pertinent questions. The trial is conducted in a cheerful Bank Holiday spirit and continues to be a great attraction.

19 Presentation of the Dunmow Flitch

Memories of the Charlbury Morris dancers, quoted by Katharine Briggs in *The Folklore of the Cotswolds,* reveal that Morris dancing used to be far from the respectable cultural activity it has now become. The team was led by a man who played the part of 'The Fool'. His wand of office was a stick with a bladder tied to one end and a calf's tail to the other. With it he kept the crowd back in order to give the dancers ample space, while keeping up a flow of wisecracks and badinage. He was the only man of the team who was paid a fee, that being regarded as compensation for keeping sober. From which one gathers that the rest of the men drank freely, which was indeed what did happen. An informed comment on the situation in the Cotswolds was that Morris dancing nearly died out because it was 'so steeped in drink and debauchery'.

Mumming plays are generally associated with Christmas, but Snowshill, in the Cotswolds, traditionally performed its version on 11 June, St Barnabas' Day, perhaps because its church is dedicated to St Barnabas. The play was similar to the usual Christmas versions in having Father Christmas as a kind of compère and in having as its main feature a duel between good (in this instance, King George), and evil (here called Bold Slasher). There is no Turkish Knight in the cast, and it is King George who gets killed.

An apparently synthetic but highly popular Whitsuntide event in the Cotswolds was the Cotswold Games, which originated in the fertile mind of one Captain Dover, who started them somewhere around the beginning of the seventeenth century. Dover was born at Barton-on-the-Heath, Warwickshire, in 1575 and became an attorney. Being 'full of activity and of a generous, free and public spirit', he petitioned King James I to be allowed to organise Whitsuntide games on a Cotswold hillside and chose for the purpose a hill now known as Dover's Hill, near Chipping Campden. The games were immensely popular and continued, with a break during the Civil War, until 1851, though in their final years they fell into disrepute because of increasing rowdiness. An old illustration depicts 'men playing at cudgels, wrestling, leaping, pitching the bar, throwing the iron hammer, handling the pyke, leaping over the heads of men kneeling, standing upon their hands, etc. Also the dancing of women, men hunting and coursing the hare with hounds and greyhounds, etc., with a castle built of boards on a hillock with guns therein.'

The Clubs which succeeded to the traditions of the Whitsun Ales and revels carried on in much the same way, though in Victorian times they gradually became less boisterous. By the 1880s most of them were conforming to a programme such as that of the Besom Club of Harnham, near Salisbury. The Club, a typical village friendly society, was so called because on parade its members carried besoms as well as the usual banners and staves. The annual festivities, on Whit Monday, began with a church service, after which the members paraded around the village, led by a brass band. They visited several public houses, had dinner at the Swan Inn and finished the day with dancing in a field. Comparatively decorous though this schedule may seem, compared with the activities of earlier centuries, there were sufficient objectionable features to arouse local hostility. *The History of Harnham,* compiled by Harnham Women's Institute, records that:

'The Rev. C.D. Crawley, who was Vicar from 1881 to 1888, did not altogether approve of so much drinking and hilarity for the children of the parish, so he used to borrow a big farm waggon from Mr Bowns, pack all the children in it, and take them up to the Race Plain for a picnic and games. But alas, as soon as he brought them home, they raced up to the field to join in that fun, too!'

At Everley, also in Wiltshire, the Whit Monday Club Fete followed a similar pattern. A fine was imposed on any members who failed to appear and a lesser fine on any who dropped out before the round of processions was completed. This was the day when villagers who had left the district made a special effort to return and meet their old friends.

Jacqueline Simpson *(The Folklore of Sussex)* records that Harting Old Club still keeps up its Whit Monday procession, as it has done since 1812. The focal point of the procession is a large beech bough, set up in the village square. The day's programme ends with a cricket match. In Cornwall there are Whitsun fairs at Helston, Lanreath and Truro.

The association of Whitsuntide with a visit to one's home parish is doubtless connected with the mediaeval custom of paying pentecostals, Whitsun farthings or smoke farthings to one's mother church at that season. The payments were originally known as Peter's Pence and were collected for despatch to Rome, but after the Reformation they were naturally kept at home. The inclusion of the word 'smoke' indicates that they were regarded as a chimney tax or hearth money. In some dioceses the smoke farthings were stored for the bishop to collect on his visitations and were used for the upkeep of the cathedral. There are many entries concerning the payment of smoke farthings in churchwardens' account books of the sixteenth and seventeenth centuries, and in Worcestershire the cathedral authorities were claiming them from parishes as late as 1825.

Village clubs seem to have been most numerous in southern England, but they were found all over the country. In Yorkshire the Club Festivals, though following the same pattern as those of the south, were held mostly on Easter Monday. The Sunday School anniversaries, which inherited some of the old Whitsun traditions on the demise of the Clubs, however, reached the climax of their efflorescence in Lancashire, notably with the Walking Days of Manchester and Salford. There the children parade, dressed in white or wearing some white article and carrying banners and bouquets of flowers. Assembled in their thousands and accompanied by many adults recapturing their own childhood, they follow a prescribed route. They are said to be so numerous that they take three or four hours to pass a given point. Whit Monday is Walking Day for the Anglican and Nonconformist children; Whit Friday for the Roman Catholics; and on the following Sunday they all have further processions in their own parishes. Similar processions take place in many places in Lancashire and Yorkshire.

Farther south, the processions are lacking, but the custom of Sunday School treats and festivities still prevails. In particular, the tradition of wearing white at Whitsun is or was widespread. In Somerset in early times women would wear white ribbon in their shoes or a white flower. In Wiltshire, Whitsuntide, rather than Easter, was the recognised time for bringing out new clothes.

In the Wiltshire village where I spent much of my life a feature of the Whitsuntide Sunday School anniversaries used, in the 1940s and 1950s, to be religious plays or tableaux. Though not of direct lineage (having been written by myself!), they were akin to the Mystery and Miracle Plays which were very popular in mediaeval England and were performed primarily at Whitsuntide, though also at other seasons. Whitsuntide was a good choice of dates, for the performances were often given in the open air, though sometimes in churches.

The outstanding examples of Whitsuntide Plays were the Chester Plays, a series of 25, which were performed in Chester annually for at least 300 years. They were presented by the city guilds, a separate play for each guild. Nine were performed on Whit Monday, nine on the Tuesday, and seven on the Wednesday. They were staged on portable platforms which were drawn about the principal streets, like floats in a modern carnival. These vehicles were two-tiered, the top floor being the stage on which the actors operated and the bottom one, screened from the public by draperies, where they changed and where the assistants produced stage effects. The programme was so arranged that a person remaining stationary at one point throughout the day would see all nine plays, in succession. All the plays dealt with Biblical themes, but the monks and others who wrote the scripts did so in the vernacular and allowed their imagination and local knowledge full liberty with the details. The crowds, which assembled in vast numbers, enjoyed them hugely, perhaps the more so because the Bishop of Chester granted a 40 days' pardon for sins to all who attended these edifying spectacles.

The decorating of churches with greenery was a part of the Whitsuntide tradition, and, for some reason, the birch was held to be particularly suitable for the purpose. Examples are recorded for Hampshire, Bedfordshire, Cambridgeshire, Herefordshire, Suffolk, Worcestershire and Shropshire. But at Kington, in Herefordshire, and Winterslow, in Wiltshire, yew was apparently the traditional tree for the purpose.

A custom associated in some places, as at Wirksworth, in Derbyshire, with Whitsuntide but more frequently with Ascensiontide is well-dressing. At Wirksworth the appointed date is Whit Wednesday. Four wells are dressed and are duly inspected by the townsfolk, who walk in procession behind a brass band. Traditionally, a short service is held at each well. Later Morris dancers perform, and the evening concludes with a fancy dress parade and dancing.

The well-dressing ceremonies that survive are concentrated mainly on Derbyshire, perhaps the best known being at Tissington. The spring-fed wells have a superstructure of stone which is decorated with flowers and greenery for the occasion. At Tissington the decorations take the form of a collage on a board panel covered with clay and surrounded by a frame. Flowers, berries, leaves, moss, lichen, fir-cones and other items of vegetation are used to build up a picture of astonishing brilliance. The subject is usually a Biblical story, and the work is executed by highly skilled craftsmen who have had years of experience. During the day clergy lead a procession to each well in turn, pronouncing a blessing on it and giving thanks for the gift of water.

The Tissington ceremony is held on Ascension Day, as are those at Buxton, Belper and other places in Derbyshire. At Buxton the Mayor and Corporation join in the procession, and a Festival Queen is crowned. At Endon, however, the customs have been transferred to 29 May and combined with the crowning of a May Queen.

Well-dressing was once much more widely practised in the midlands. There are references to it in Staffordshire, Lincolnshire and Worcestershire, among other places. In Cheshire a salt pit at Nantwich was similarly dressed on Ascension Day until about 1750.

Tissington has a tradition that its well-dressing ceremony began in 1350 to

20 Well-Dressing at Tissington, Derbyshire

commemorate its immunity from the Black Death in the previous year. With some justification its inhabitants ascribed their escape to the purity of the water from their five wells. The idea is a worthy one, but in all probability the custom is much older.

In pagan times the nymphs and goddesses of wells and springs were worshipped throughout Europe, as the literature of Greece and Rome testifies. Celtic imagination ensured that Britain was liberally peopled by such fairy spirits. It is not without significance that holy wells were and are particularly numerous in Celtic Cornwall. As so often happened, the Christian church took over traditions and customs too strong to be abolished, in Cornwall the wells being allocated to one or another of the numerous obscure Cornish saints.

Here, too, there is an association with Ascensiontide. The well at St Cubert, for instance, the water of which was held to cure cripples, was effective only on Ascension Day. The water in Chapel Uny Well, Sancreed, would heal wounds only on the first three Wednesdays of May. In north Devon the water from holy wells at North Molton, Hatherleigh and elsewhere had its most potent curative properties if collected early in the morning of Ascension Day. At Burnham, near Haxey, Lincolnshire, children were dipped in the holy well there on Ascension Day, to be cured of deformities and skin diseases. Water from holy wells was also used for divination, people trying to discern their fate from the behaviour of pins, needles or pebbles thrown in. That this superstition is by no means dead is evident from the pennies and other coins thrown into any pool labelled 'Wishing Well'. People will even toss coins, for luck, into ornamental pools in short-lived horticultural shows.

The curative properties of water from holy wells on Ascension Day were extended to rainwater which fell on that day. It was held to be particularly effective in treating sore eyes.

At Shaftesbury, Dorset, until 1830 a ceremony connected with water rights was held annually on Ascension Day. Apparently this ancient hill-top borough depended for its water supply on three or four wells at Enmore Green, at the foot of the hill, the water being carried up on horse panniers or on people's heads. Enmore Green was in the manor of Gillingham, so the burgesses of Shaftesbury had to pay a tribute to the lord of the manor of Gillingham for the privilege of using the wells. This took the form of a calf's head, a pair of gloves, a gallon of ale, two penny loaves of wheaten bread and an elaborate May garland, decorated with peacock feathers and gold, which was known locally as a 'besom'. On Ascension Day the Mayor of Shaftesbury had to go in procession to Enmore Green to hand over these gifts to the steward of Gillingham Manor. The besom was duly restored to him and carried back to Shaftesbury. A good deal of pageantry was involved, with a Lord and Lady taking leading parts.

Another curious Ascensiontide custom is preserved at Boyes Staith, near Whitby, Yorkshire, where a hedge has to be erected on the beach on the eve of Ascension Day. This commemorates a mediaeval penance imposed by the Abbot of Whitby on some local noblemen who disturbed a holy hermit at his prayers and beat him up. The stakes and osiers for the hedge had to be cut in a local wood at sunrise on Ascension Eve, carried to Whitby Harbour at low tide and made into a hedge strong enough to stand three full tides.

Combe Martin in north Devon had an Ascensiontide custom which combined typical May Day celebrations, including Hobby Horse and Fool, with a local legend. An extract from my book, *The Folklore of Devon,* summarises the festivities of 'The Hunting of the Earl of Rone', which continued until around 1837:

'On the afternoon of Ascension Day the villagers, wearing their best clothes, marched to Lady's Wood to search for the Earl. They were led by a party of men dressed as Grenadiers. After spending some time looking in every unlikely spot they found the Earl lurking in some undergrowth. They fired a volley and then, surrounding the prisoner, set him, face to tail, on a donkey decorated with garlands of flowers and a necklace of twelve sea-biscuits. The Earl and the other characters in the procession, notably the Fool and the Hobby-Horse, wore grotesque masks. The Fool carried a broom and a bucket of dirty water. The Hobby-Horse had realistic jaws, that worked mechanically and was known as "the mapper", perhaps a corruption of "snapper", for the Horse capered along, snapping at the spectators.

At intervals along the route the Grenadiers, who wore tall paper hats adorned with ribbons, halted and fired a volley, whereupon the Earl fell off his donkey, wounded. The grief-stricken Fool and Hobby-Horse attempted to cure him. For the rest of the time they collected money from the crowd. Anyone refusing to contribute was either sprinkled with dirty water by the Fool, or seized by the Hobby-Horse, or both. The procession made its way to the sea-shore but was a long time getting there, for, as a nineteenth-century writer points out, ''refreshments were taken en route, and the rate of progress varied inversely as the number of public-houses along the line of march''.'

The occasion obviously contained elements of several different traditions, among them a mumming play, for the wounding of the Earl and the attempts to cure him are clearly reminiscent of the basic plot in all such plays. The Combe Martin event was said to commemorate the capture of the Earl of Tyrone, who, in Elizabethan times, landed nearby as a political refugee. He lived for some days in the woods, existing on ships' biscuits which he wore around his neck as a necklace. That, at least, is the local version of the affair.

There can be no doubt that the restoration of Charles II to the throne in 1660 was popular. The squabbling sectaries who tried to exercise control of the state after the death of Cromwell made such a poor showing that the country in general was glad to be rid of them. The people were tired of experiment and glad to return to the old ways. It seemed natural to keep the date of Charles's accession as a holiday, and the date was near enough to May Day to attract many of the old Maytime customs, now enthusiastically revived. The romantic story of Charles's escape after the Battle of Worcester by hiding in the Boscobel Oak suggested an association with the oldtime festival of the greenwood. Wearing a sprig of oak became a royalist badge. The Royal Oak was adopted as a sign by innumerable public houses, and Oak Apple Day became an occasion for annual rejoicing. Maypoles were erected, the Queen of the May made her appearance once again, the Morris dancers revived their ancient skill, and rural England became merry again.

Ceremonies and traditions associated with the cult of the oak seem to have been automatically transferred to Oak Apple Day. Christina Hole (*English Custom and Usage*) describes how at Whitchurch Canonicorum, Dorset, the villagers went to the woods at three o'clock in the morning to cut oak branches. One of the largest boughs was hauled to the top of the church tower, another was set up on a post in the middle of the village, while lesser ones were used to decorate the porches of houses. Writing in 1941, Miss Hole adds that the custom had not long died out, and at Wishford, Wiltshire, almost exactly the same procedure is followed on Oak Apple Day, as described on pages 70-72.

To generations of children in many parts of the country Oak Apple Day was Pinch-Bum Day, the loyal youngsters who wore sprigs of oak regarding it as their bounden duty to pinch the bums of those who did not. A legend explains the custom by asserting that when Charles II was hiding in the Boscobel Oak one of his companions had to keep pinching him to prevent him from falling asleep when

his pursuers were near, but obviously the practice had so much to commend it to the participants that a legend was hardly needed. Alternatives to pinching recalcitrants who refused to sport an oak spray were many and varied. They included (a) beating them with nettles, (b) spitting on them, (c) pelting them with birds' eggs and addled hens' eggs, (d) kicking them and (e) drenching them with water. In some districts it was necessary to wear the oak only until noon; after that one was safe. In others, oak leaves were not sufficient, one had to find a sprig with an oak apple on it. The custom was widely observed throughout England, from Cumberland to Cornwall. In some places a kind of secrecy was involved. At Whippingham, on the Isle of Wight, the spray of oak had to be concealed until the bearer was challenged with the words,

The twenty-ninth of May
Is Oak Apple Day.

He then had to reveal his oak token, and woe betide him if he had forgotten it. At Wishford, Wiltshire, a prize is given for the oak branch with the greatest number of oak apples. A name formerly applied widely to Oak Apple Day was 'Shick-shack Day', the oak apples being known as 'shick-shacks'. In parts of Somerset anyone who did not wear the oak leaf or oak apple on 29 May was called a 'Jick-jack'.

The custom, already noted in connection with Whitchurch Canonicorum and Wishford, of hauling a big oak bough to the tower of the parish church on Oak Apple Day was formerly also observed in a number of other places, in Hampshire, Cheshire, Buckinghamshire, Worcestershire, Herefordshire and elsewhere. The church bells were rung at six o'clock in the morning, and there seems to have been a widespread belief that until that hour on 29 May people were at liberty to go into woods and forests and cut green wood freely. Houses were decorated with green branches, and so was the harness of horses — again in many parts of the country. In the nineteenth century the practice of decking out horses in greenery seems to have been transferred to steam locomotives as well as to stations, signal boxes and other railway buildings. At Castleton, on the Isle of Man, the practice of decorating the church tower with oak boughs was improved on by substituting an enormous and elaborate garland for the oak branch. It consisted of masses of flowers attached to a wooden frame, the whole weighing more than a hundredweight. The celebrations associated with the occasion included Morris dancers, a band and a king and queen on horseback leading a procession, the 'queen' being a man in woman's clothing. The making of garlands was also observed in other places, including Gainsborough and Upton-on-Severn, evidently having been transferred to 29 May from May Day. At Tavistock, Devon, the garlands took the form of two crossed hoops, wreathed with flowers and acting as a frame for a string of birds' eggs. Children spent the previous week or two collecting as many eggs as possible, chiefly those of blackbirds and thrushes but strictly refraining from taking robins' eggs. Gaily dressed and sporting oak leaves, they paraded around the town with their garlands, collecting pennies from door to

21 Oak Apple Day at Wishford, Wiltshire. The banners advertise the villagers' rights to cut green wood in Grovely Forest

door. In the afternoon they used the garlands as Aunt Sallies, each child trying to smash as many eggs as possible. The robbing of the birds' nest was known as 'halfing'.

Tavistock, like several other Devonshire towns, was the scene of mock battles between Roundheads and Cavaliers on Oak Apple Day until apparently about the middle of the nineteenth century. At Tiverton, where the fights were exceptionally furious, King Charles was represented, at least on some occasions, by a small boy dressed in white, while Cromwell was 'the biggest ruffian that Tiverton could produce; his face was covered with a mixture of oil and lamp-black, and round his waist was tied a bag containing a similar mixture, with which he treated the face of anyone who was caught by him and refused to pay the ransom demanded from him'. Pitched battles were fought in the streets by the supporters of the two heroes, but the aim was rather to take prisoners than to break heads. The ransom money was needed for evening carousals in the public houses.

A somewhat similar gang war was staged in Exeter on Oak Apple Day, though apparently no attempt was made to identify the rival armies with Roundheads and Cavaliers. The day was known locally as 'Lawless Day', by invocation of the false argument that on certain days the law is powerless. A feature of the Exeter proceedings was the damming of the open drains that ran through the streets. When a sufficiently large pool of dirty water had collected, an ambush was laid for passers-by, who were given the choice of paying a ransom or being ducked in or splashed with the muddy water.

One further Maytime festival was Rogationtide. The Rogation days are properly the Monday, Tuesday and Wednesday before Ascension Day, the preceding Sunday being Rogation Sunday. A name applied to them in some parts of the kingdom was the 'Gange Days', 'gange' being derived from the same root as 'going'. It is likely that Rogationtide customs had their origin with festivities connected with the Roman god Terminus, the god of fields and landmarks.

One aspect of Rogationtide is well illustrated by its modern revival in many parishes. The congregations of the various churches in the parish unite in a procession which takes them to certain key stations, such as the village green, the village hall, the school, a garden, a meadow, a cultivated field and so on. At each station a hymn is sung and prayer offered, the proceedings ending with a short service in the parish church. Blessings are thus pronounced on all the main activities of a rural village.

For many centuries this concept of Rogationtide was combined with the utilitarian idea of memorising the boundaries of the parish. The procession then progressed around the perimeter of the parish rather than visiting the main centres of activity. The people taking part were armed with long rods, with which they 'beat the bounds' — at least, in more recent times. In earlier ages it was the children who were soundly beaten when key points were reached. The exercise was doubtless valuable in days before maps were in general use, and a sound thrashing was one way of impressing a locality on a child's mind. Other methods of ensuring that landmarks were faithfully remembered included throwing victims into a

22 Oak Apple Day in Castleton, Derbyshire

23 Children Beating the Bounds of St Michael's parish, Oxford

24 Beating the Bounds, Canterbury

bramble hedge, ducking them and beating their backsides with a shovel while they were standing on their heads in a hole. Numerous Gospel Oaks in various parts of Britain are a reminder of trees under which the gospel was once read on Rogation Days.

Perambulating the boundaries of a rural parish could be a protracted and exacting procedure, involving as it did crosscountry rambles where often no path existed. With the twentieth-century amalgamation of parishes it would be an even lengthier business. It was undertaken in 1976 in the downland parishes of the Deverill valley in west Wiltshire, where five former parishes have been combined into one, but as the perimeter is now 12 miles the parishioners went to key points by car. Enid Porter, in *The Folklore of East Anglia,* records that during the millenary celebrations of Ely Cathedral in 1973 'the task of beating the bounds of the entire diocese was undertaken by the Bishops of Ely and Huntingdon'.

Known as the 'Midsummer Tithes', though it has nothing to do with Midsummer, a curious Rogationtide custom is preserved at Wishford, Wiltshire. Just before sunset on Rogation Monday the grazing and grass-cutting rights on two riverside meadows are sold by auction in the church porch. The parish clerk conducts the auction, using the church key as a hammer, and the rights are knocked down to the last bidder at the moment of sunset.

The custom of auctioning grazing and grass-cutting rights is widespread and common in the West Country, particularly in lowland Somerset and north Dorset, but most of the sales are held in April, and I know of no other firm links with Rogationtide.

CHAPTER 7

Midsummer

AGRICULTURALLY, June is one of the busier months. The two main activities are hay-making and sheep-shearing, except in the north, where these two operations are often delayed until July. There is thus less time for festivals and merry-making than in May.

Ecclesiastically, too, June is an undistinguished month. Since England became a Protestant country and so lost the feast of Corpus Christi, the chief dates in the Church calendar are Trinity Sunday and the feast days of Saints Barnabas, John the Baptist and Peter, though sometimes Whitsuntide falls in June. Trinity Sunday is the Sunday after Whitsuntide and has the distinction that the next 27 Sundays are reckoned from it. There are now no other major landmarks in the calendar of the Church of England until we come to Advent. The last Sunday of November is the Twenty-seventh Sunday after Trinity, the first Sunday of December is the First Sunday in Advent. Of the saints, St Barnabas has his feast-day on 11 June, St John the Baptist on 24 June, and St Peter on 29 June.

Of them all the Feast of St John the Baptist is probably the most significant, because it inherited the vestiges of a number of ancient celebrations associated with Midsummer, and the Eve is as important as the Feast Day. Although not one of the Celtic quarter days, Midsummer was a festival of great importance in the lives of the inhabitants of our islands 2000 years ago; and in an earlier age, too, for it is well known and has been scientifically established that the axis of Stonehenge, erected between 1800 and 1400 B.C., is orientated towards the sunrise at the summer solstice (21 June). It would seem that early man was intensely preoccupied with the celestial bodies and that the longest day, when the sun reached its highest point in the heavens, had considerable significance for him.

In his account of his campaign in Gaul in the first century B.C. Julius Caesar noted, in a much quoted passage, that it was the custom of certain Celtic tribes, under the influence of Druids, to construct gigantic figures of wickerwork, fill them with human beings (stated to be criminals) and burn them as a sacrifice. The name of the god thus honoured was apparently Taranis. The theory that these holocausts were the origin of the numerous associations of bonfires with Midsummer has been popular with antiquarians, especially in the eighteenth and nineteenth centuries, when the bonfire traditions were more widely maintained. J. Brand *(Observations on Popular Antiquities)* gives examples of survivals of bonfire customs in Cornwall, Devon, Gloucestershire, Eton, Northumberland and several parts of Ireland. He quotes an eyewitness account, from the *Gentleman's Magazine* of February 1795, of the Midsummer bonfires in 1782 in an unnamed Irish locality:

'At the house where I was entertained it was told me that we should see at midnight the most singular sight in Ireland, which was the lighting of Fires in honour of the Sun. Accordingly, exactly at midnight, the Fires began to appear; and, taking advantage of going up to the leads of the house, which had a widely extended view, I saw on a radius of thirty miles all around the Fires burning on every eminence which the country afforded. I had a farther satisfaction in learning, from an undoubted authority, that the people danced round the Fires, and at the close went through these fires, and made their sons and daughters together with their cattle pass through the Fire; and the whole was conducted with religious solemnity.'

Brand quotes another writer (of 1723) to the effect that, again in Ireland, 'On the vigil of St John the Baptist's Nativity they make Bonfires and run along the streets and fields with wisps of straw blazing on long poles to purify the air, which they think infected, by believing all the devils, spirits, ghosts and hobgoblins fly abroad this night to hurt mankind.'

He mentions, too, that in Northumberland and Cumberland it was the custom to make bonfires 'on the tops of high hills and in the villages and sport and dance around them.' Marjorie Rowling *(The Folklore of the Lake District)* states that at Wetheral, in Cumberland, Midsummer Wakes were held on the common until well into the nineteenth century. Here again, features of the festival were a huge bonfire and the bearing of blazing torches around the village. As elsewhere, most of the old fire customs, some of them formerly associated with other seasons of the year, have now been concentrated on Guy Fawkes' Night.

In Cornwall the Midsummer Bonfire custom was revived in 1929 by the Old Cornwall Movement and now flourishes. The bonfires form a chain on the hill-tops from Carn Brea, between Redruth and Camborne, and the eastern borders of Bodmin Moor. Tony Deane and Tony Shaw *(The Folklore of Cornwall)* give a detailed account of the celebrations, mentioning that sometimes young couples leap through the flames, for good luck. Various herbs and a newly-cut oak bough are thrown on the fire. At an earlier date cattle, although they were not driven through the flames, had brands of burning gorse passed over them. The farmers who carried the torches were always careful to walk sunwise. The occasion was also marked by bouts of that favourite Cornish sport, wrestling.

The bonfire tradition has also been revived in Devon, where the fires are lit on the high tors, though popular belief is that they commemorate the beacon fires that gave warning of the approach of the Spanish Armada.

Doris Jones-Baker *(The Folklore of Hertfordshire)* records that Midsummer Eve bonfires were once lit along the crests of the Chiltern Hills, the village of Hexton still possessing its 'Bonfirehill Knoll'. Old people at Bishop's Stortford in 1904 could just remember when the bonfires were lit annually.

At Whalton, in Northumberland, the custom of the Midsummer Bonfire has never been dropped and, quite remarkably, it is celebrated on 4 July, which is the Eve of Midsummer Day, Old Style, according to the pre-1752 calendar.

The dancing around the Midsummer Bonfire should always be done clockwise, that means following the sun on his journey from east to west across the heavens. The occasion is, of course, a reminder of the circling of the year. From this point onwards the day length will gradually decline until Midwinter Day, when the long climb back to warmth and light in the northern hemisphere begins. The dedication of the festival to John the Baptist was held to be particularly appropriate by reason of John's pronouncement when referring to Christ, 'He must increase, and I must decrease.'

It is tempting to conjecture whether the giants associated in so many instances with Midsummer festivities have their origin in those wickerwork giants recorded by Caesar. Certainly giants play a prominent part in Midsummer folklore.

Salisbury has a magnificent effigy of a giant, 12 feet high and with dark, semi-negroid features and a black, bushy beard, who is said to represent St Christopher. He is domiciled in Salisbury Museum and now appears in the streets only on special occasions, as in processions for jubilees and coronations, but formerly he paraded at least once annually, on Midsummer Day. That was because Midsummer Day was the patronal festival of the mediaeval Tailors' Guild, which had appropriated the Giant as a kind of mascot, but knowledgeable writers have suspected that he belongs to an earlier tradition and had a long previous association with Midsummer.

Dancing around the bonfire was an important feature in the Midsummer celebrations in the Orkneys and Shetlands, and in *The Folklore of Orkney and Shetland* Ernest W. Marwick says that 'jumping through the flames seems to have been essential everywhere'. In the eighteenth century it was the custom to walk several times around the fire, going in a clockwise direction. Blazing brands were used to encircle houses and fields and also cattle in their stalls, the treatment being held especially effective in curing sterility in cows.

In Sunderland the custom of leaping through the flames of a Midsummer bonfire was transferred to the streets of the town, where fires were made of coal, tar-barrels and any other material that happened to be available. In the middle of the nineteenth century memories still survived among old people in Nottinghamshire and Derbyshire of 'Belfires' on Midsummer Eve or Midsummer

Night, again accompanied by leaping and dancing. At the end of the century Midsummer fires, with the appropriate feast and revelry, were still remembered as having taken place each year in the market place of Richmond, Yorkshire.

Burford is another town which formerly had a Midsummer giant. Just as the Salisbury giant is accompanied by a grotesque, snapping effigy known as the Hobnob, so the Burford giant had a companion dragon. The local tradition, for what it is worth, was that the dragon commemorated a victory by the West Saxons over the Mercians there at some time in the Dark Ages. Giant and dragon paraded twice a year, at Whitsuntide and again at Midsummer, which was, of course, St John's Day, and John the Baptist happened to be the patron saint of the town.

In *The Folklore of the Welsh Border* Jacqueline Simpson recalls that Chester staged a Midsummer pageant until in 1599 a Puritan mayor, Henry Hardware, 'caused the giants in the Midsomer Show to be put downe and broken . . . the Devil in his feathers which rode for the Butchers he put away, and the cuppes and cannes, and the Dragon and Naked Boys . . .' The pageant possessed, before this, no fewer than four giants, as well as 'a unicorn, a dromedary, a camel, a luce, an ass, a dragon, six hobby horses and six naked boys'. Some of the items, notably the Dragon, appeared briefly in a revival of the old tradition after the Restoration, but it was only temporary.

Brand *(Observations on Popular Antiquities)* quotes several mediaeval references to giants in Midsummer celebrations in London. One, from 1589,

25 Belfire Tenders at Whalton, Northumberland, 1903

speaks of 'great and uglie Gyants, marching as if they were alive and armed at all points, but within they are stuffed full of browne paper and tow . . . .'Edinburgh, too, apparently had a giant, though contemporary records (of the sixteenth century) call it an idol or 'an ald stok-image'. At Norwich the Tuesday before Midsummer Day was known as Snapdragon Day, because then the effigy of a dragon was carried in a procession led by the mayor of the city. A similar figure features in a St John the Baptist Day procession at Wymondham, also in Norfolk.

At Chester the traditional pageantry of the festival took the form of performances of the celebrated Chester Mystery Plays. These plays, originally associated with Corpus Christi, became well known in many other parts of England, and a record of 1575 notes that the Lord Mayor of London 'caused the Popish Plays of Chester to be played on the Sunday, Monday, Tuesday and Wednesday after Midsummer Day'.

References to the lads and lasses of Orkney and Shetland dancing around their bonfires right through the night may serve to remind us that in those high latitudes darkness never falls at Midsummer; there is throughout the night a soft twilight and a rim of light along the northern and eastern horizon. Farther south, the tradition of keeping vigil all through the night was also widespread.

This book is specifically concerned with *country* customs, and the giants, processions and mystery plays have brought us into the town. The towns in mediaeval times were, of course, not the urban monsters familiar to us today but were modest nuclei of what may perhaps fairly be described as concentrated squalor. Congested though they were, they were small and hence easily accessible to country lads escaping from their fields on a festival day. We can imagine that there was a fair sprinkling of village folk in the crowds that watched the Chester Plays at Midsummer. If the performances of the Plays given in London in 1575 were repeated ten years later it is likely that they were seen by William Shakespeare, newly arrived from the country and ready to have his imagination fired by them.

Early in the same century the 'marching watches' of London reached their zenith. Evidently there was an ancient tradition of keeping watch on Midsummer Eve, and the older version of the custom is referred to as the 'standing watch'. However, even at Midsummer it can be rather chilly in the small hours, so we can understand that watchers would prefer to move around. In London by the time of Henry VIII the procession was said to number 2000 persons, led by watchmen holding, as torches, fire-baskets on long poles. Evidently the general populace joined in, and the nobility came along at first to watch and later to take part. King Henry himself attended a marching watch incognito in 1510 and was so enthusiastic about what he saw that a few nights later (on St Peter's Eve, when the procession was repeated), he came with his queen and a bevy of courtiers to grace the occasion. There being little chance of sleep on such a night, householders set tables outside their doors and served refreshments for themselves and their neighbours. Records of similar junketings also exist for Nottingham, and it is unlikely that the custom was confined to these two towns.

And what was the purpose of the 'watch'? At Nottingham it seems to have been associated with defence, the keeping of 'watch and ward' over the city. The watchmen who formed the nucleus of the procession, about 200 of them, paraded armed and took an oath that 'they shall well and truly keep this town until tomorrow at the sunrising'. They patrolled the streets with military precision but, on the other hand, they each wore a garland of flowers and ribbons and whatever other finery they could lay hands on, which would seem somewhat frivolous for a military exercise. Besides, the 'watch and ward' theory leaves unexplained why the custom was confined to Midsummer Eve.

Back to the countryside, where most of these ancient customs had their roots. There we find the belief, apparently very widespread in remote antiquity, that on Midsummer Eve the spirits of the living leave their mortal bodies and wander freely. In particular they visit the spot where, in due course, they will quit their body permanently. It follows that they are interested in their decease and anything connected with it, which naturally includes the church and graveyard.

The tradition thus arose that anyone who had the temerity to sit in the church porch all through the night of Midsummer Eve would see pass before him, in procession, all those souls in the parish who would die within the next year, parading in order of decease. Many localities developed their own refinements of the tradition. In some it was held that vigil had to be kept not in the porch but in some spot from which the porch could be clearly seen. In others, watch had to be kept for three successive years before the vision was granted. The Rev. George Tyzack, in his *Lore and Legend of the English Church*, records the pragmatic approach to the matter displayed by a Yorkshire sexton who regularly kept vigil at his church on Midsummer Eve in order to calculate his income from grave-digging in the coming year!

Obviously one's spirit could leave one's body and go a-wandering only if one were asleep, which was another good reason for keeping awake all through the witching hours of Midsummer Eve. It was said that if a watcher keeping vigil at the church himself fell asleep, that was a sure sign that he would be one of the casualties in the next 12 months.

To appreciate the atmosphere in which our ancestors lived their lives it is necessary to enter, as far as we are able, into their beliefs about the dual nature of the world. For them there were two planes of existence — the visible, tangible world of the daylight and the invisible, mysterious world of the night. The latter was peopled by ghosts, witches and spirits of all kinds, many of them malevolent. At certain times the nebulous frontier between the two realms wore very thin, and adventurous souls might pass through. (The unadventurous shut their windows tight and longed for the morning.) Midsummer Eve was one of those times, and, as we have already noted, St Mark's Eve (24 April) was another, with Hallowe'en being the prime example.

Arising from these beliefs are the superstitions regarding fern seed. The thinking behind them is that as the spores of ferns are so tiny as to be practically invisible and yet obviously exist — for they give life to new ferns — therefore anyone who gathered fern seeds in the proper manner at the appropriate magic hour would acquire from them the cloak of invisibility. The possession of such a gift was particularly valuable on Midsummer Eve, as the fern seed also gave immunity from the power of witches, spirits in general and the Devil himself. Thus fortified, a man might wander at will in the Otherworld.

On a more practical level, he might also spy on his lady love, a consideration which doubtless prompted many young men to try to obtain the magic seed. Records refer specifically to 'young men' embarking on such expeditions. It seems that the most effective method of catching the seed was to surround the ferns with pewter plates and then, at midnight on Midsummer Eve, to shake the fronds so that the spores fell on the plates. But one had to be both vigilant and lucky, for the Devil resented humans acquiring such supernatural powers and did his best to prevent it.

In Sussex they had the circumvention of the Devil worked out in detail. At seven o'clock on Midsummer Day you walk up to Chanctonbury Ring and run seven times around the hill-top clump of trees. The Devil will then appear and offer you a bowl of soup or porridge. This you refuse, and thereafter he has no power over you. Some versions of the recipe specify midnight instead of seven o'clock; others say any moonless night will do; and one stipulates that you must run backwards!

Unmarried girls had a different reason for seeking to penetrate into the Unknown. They wanted to know the identity of their future husband. Here again the magic fern seed could help. It had to be scattered at midnight while the maiden recited,

> *Fern seed I sow,*
> *Fern seed I hoe,*
> *In hopes my true love will come after me and mow.*

In some versions she has to do this as she runs three times round the church while the clock is striking midnight. As she finishes she will see, if she glances over her shoulder, the wraith of her future husband following her and mowing with a scythe.

Other versions alter 'fern seed' to 'hemp seed'. This tradition has been recorded in Sussex, Cornwall, Devon, Herefordshire, Oxfordshire, Norfolk and perhaps in other counties as well. As hemp seed is better known today as cannabis, one is inclined to wonder just what was the part it played in these old-time practices.

Several other plants were used in Midsummer divinations, among them St John's-wort, vervain, rose, trefoil, orpine and mugwort. St John's-wort, of course, owes its name to its dedication in monastic lore to St John the Baptist. At Midsummer it was hung around the doors and windows of houses to ward off evil spirits, and in some parts of the country sprigs of its were worn in buttonholes or on hats.

So too was Orpine, a fleshy-leaved plant with a rosette of pink flowers which bloom at this season. An alternative name for Orpine is Livelong, a reference to the length of time that stalks of it will remain fresh and green when used for decorating houses. Possibly because of this characteristic it was associated with fidelity. A girl wishing to know whether her lover would be faithful to her would place two plants, one for the girl and one for the boy, side by side on a plate or hang them side by side in her room. If they bent towards each other all would be well; if they bent away, he would jilt her; if his withered and died, they would never be married. The plant was also known as Midsummer Men.

Mugwort, an unattractive plant little regarded nowadays, was valued because of the belief that beneath its roots could sometimes be found a piece of coal with magical properties. One version of the tradition says that it can only be found at noon on Midsummer Day. Taken home and placed under the pillow at night, it will ensure that the girl sleeping there will dream of her future husband. Another version says that the coal must be dug up at midnight on Midsummer Eve. The 'coal' is actually a decayed part of the root.

A rose plucked at Midsummer will, it was said in Devon, last fresh until Christmas. The girl who had picked it should then wear it to church, when her lover would come and take it from her. This superstition was also known in Cornwall and Worcestershire. Again there would seem to be an association between the long life of the rose and the fidelity of the sweetheart. A Somerset tradition substitutes 'rose leaves' for 'hemp seed' or 'fern seed' in the rhyme quoted above.

Another form of divination associated with Midsummer was for a girl to turn a clean chemise inside out, damp it and hang it over the back of a chair before the fire. This had to be done in complete silence. The girl's future husband would then enter and turn the chemise. Unless pre-arrangements had been made, this would seem an improbable sequence of events.

In addition to the general folklore connected with Midsummer a number of localities preserve particular associations. One such is the megalithic monument of Stanton Drew in the county of Avon (formerly Somerset). The local legend purporting to explain the origin of the stones, which form three circles, a semi-circular group and one menhir, is as follows:

A wedding party assembled in a field at Stanton Drew for an outdoor feast and dance. At midnight, when the revelry was at its height, the fiddler to whose playing they were dancing, broke off and reminded the dancers that it was now the Sabbath. He refused to play any more, despite the anger of the bride, who declared that she would have music even if she had to go to hell for it. Whereupon an old man appeared and offered to take the fiddler's place. The dance proceeded and grew faster and faster. When the dancers begged the musician to ease off he took no notice, and while he kept playing they felt compelled to continue dancing. By daybreak they were exhausted. As the cock crew the fiddler departed, and the dancers were turned to stone. This happened on Midsummer Eve. The story is said to have been related by the devout fiddler who refused to play on a Sunday but who hid under a hedge during the subsequent proceedings and saw everything that happened. Locally the stones are still known as 'The Devil's Wedding', or 'The Fiddlers and the Maids'.

The Rollright Stones in Oxfordshire are also reputed to be men turned to stone. Here the men were a king and his knights who once set out to conquer England. At Rollright they were met by a witch who told the king to take seven long strides and if, at the seventh, he could see the village of Long Compton, in the valley beneath the hill where the encounter was taking place, he would become king of England. This seemed to him an easy task, but as he was taking the seventh stride a long barrow (tumulus) rose suddenly out of the ground and obscured his view. Whereupon he and his knights were turned to stone, while the witch, after a tradition much favoured by witches, became an elder tree.

The event presumably occurred on Midsummer Eve, for thereafter it was celebrated on that date. People used to make a pilgrimage there and stand in a circle around the 'King Stone', while one man cut a branch off the elder tree. At this, the tree bled, and the King Stone 'moved its head'. The occasion was celebrated with dancing and with refreshments of cake and ale. At times the 'knights' were said to whisper to each other, and girls seeking to know the future of their love affairs used to creep up and try to overhear what they were saying. Fairies also used to emerge from a hole in the ground near the King Stone and dance around the stone circle.

Fairies are said to dance, too, at various places on the South Downs in Sussex on Midsummer Eve. It may be significant that one, Harrow Hill near Patching, has prehistoric flint-mines, while two others, Cissbury and Tarberry Hill, have notable hill-top earthworks. On the same range of downs, near Broadwater, a party of skeletons was said to emerge from beneath the roots of an old oak tree on Midsummer Eve and to dance around the tree till dawn, scaring the wits out of anyone who happened to see them.

Cornish witches used to meet on Midsummer Eve on a rock known as 'The Witches' Rock' near Zennor. Anyone bold enough to venture there at midnight and touch the rock nine times would have good luck. At the other end of Britain, in the Shetland Isles, seals, who were supposed to be bewitched human beings, were said to slough off their skins and become human again on Midsummer Eve. They spent the short night dancing on lonely sea-rocks until daybreak compelled them to resume their usual form. An old tradition in Sussex averred that cattle go down on their knees at midnight on Midsummer Eve, presumably worshipping.

Appleton, in Cheshire, has an old custom known as 'Bawming the Thorn', 'bawming' or 'barning' meaning decorating or anointing. The thorn in question is a young hawthorn, planted in 1967 to replace one that had been blown down, but its predecessor is said to have been grown from a cutting of the Glastonbury Thorn. On Old Midsummer Day (5 July) the tree is adorned with ribbons, flags, garlands and whatever flowers are obtainable. Formerly a village festival was associated with the ceremony, but in recent years it has been revived as a children's occasion.

The event looks like a maypole festival transferred from May Day to Old

Midsummer, but it seems more likely to be a survival of a once widespread tradition of decorating trees and other features at Midsummer. Brand *(Observations on Popular Antiquities)* quotes a writer, date unspecified, who notes that on passing through Little Brickhill, in Buckinghamshire, on Midsummer Eve he found every signpost in the town decorated with green birch. He also gives examples from churchwardens' accounts in London parishes for 'birch at Midsummer'. Earlier we have noted that houses were decorated with St John's-wort and other flowers, and Stow, in his *Survey of London* (1598), comments:

> 'On the vigil of St John Baptist every man's door being shadowed with green birch, long fennel, St John's-wort, orpin, white lilies and suchlike, garnished upon with garlands of beautiful flowers, had also lamps of glass, with oil burning in them all the night; some hung out branches of iron curiously wrought, containing hundreds of lamps alight at once, which made a goodly show.'

At Magdalen College, Oxford, a sermon is preached on St John's Day (24 June) from a stone pulpit in the quadrangle. The custom dates from the time when, before the founding of the college, a hospital dedicated to St John the Baptist stood on the site, and there was an old tradition, now discontinued, that 'a large fence of green boughs' had to be erected around the quadrangle for the occasion. It was said that this was to represent John the Baptist preaching in the wilderness, but it is more likely to have been part of the general decorations for Midsummer.

Probably connected with the same almost universal tradition of Midsummer was the northern custom, recorded for Northumberland and Durham by Brand, of creating cushions of flowers and exhibiting them in the streets. 'A layer of clay', says Brand, 'was placed on the stool, and therein was stuck, with great regularity, an arrangement of all kinds of flowers, so close as to form a beautiful cushion.' Those who made and paraded these cushions did so in order to collect alms 'to enable them to have an evening feast and dancing'.

The ceremony of 'Clipping the Church', meaning to join hands and dance around it, was in some places associated with Midsummer, though in other places with Shrove Tuesday and other seasons. It seems probable that the custom has a pagan origin, the church substituting for a former sacred site with possibly a sacred standing stone to be danced around. Midsummer, with its associations with the circling sun, would seem an appropriate date for the ceremony.

Devon had a tradition of 'Dancing Trees', around which villagers danced and feasted on festival days. In several instances they danced not around them but *on* them! Examples include trees at Dunsford, Lifton, Trebursaye, Meavy and Moretonhampstead. An account of the Meavy Oak describes how this was done:

> 'This tree till within this century was, on the village festival, surrounded with poles, a platform erected above the tree, the top of which was kept clipped flat, like a table, and a set of stairs erected, by means of which the platform could be reached. On the top a table and chairs were placed, and feasting took place.'

A similar arrangement was made at the Cross Tree, a pollarded elm, at Moretonhampstead, on which, it was said, there was 'sufficient room for thirty persons to sit around and six couples to dance, besides the orchestra'. Though these trees were used for all or most village festivals, Midsummer Day was certainly one such occasion in some villages.

At Cornish village festivals the election of a Mock Mayor was a common feature. The 'mayor' presided over festivities, which frequently lasted a week, and imbibed large quantities of free ale. At the end he had to pay for it all by being unceremoniously dunked in a muddy pond or in the sea, but by that time he was usually too drunk to care. Two places in which these revels took place on or near Midsummer were Pelynt and Polperro, the actual date for Polperro being 29 June, St Peter's Day, St Peter being the village's patron saint.

Cricklade, in Wiltshire, had around this date a Tanbark Festival, marking the end of the season for stripping the bark from oak trees for use in tanneries. Evidently a considerable number of the town's inhabitants were employed in this industry, and the Festival seems to have taken the form of a Harvest Home feast, with a good deal of drinking and conviviality. Parts of a play written for performance on this occasion and resembling in some respects a mumming play are still extant.

In some places the Midsummer celebrations spilled over, in the course of time, to the adjacent festivals of St Peter (29 June) and St Paul (30 June). St Peter's Day is, naturally, associated with fishermen. Wendy Boase in *The Folklore of Hampshire and the Isle of Wight* says that the millpond at Fareham used to be drained each year on this date, the eels and other fish left floundering in the mud being fair game for anyone who could catch them. Until the end of the eighteenth century the fishermen of Itchen used to carry an image of St Peter in procession on that day.

Midsummer was also a special festival for Cornish tin-miners, who used to have a paid half-holiday for celebrations. The conventional bonfires formed an important part of the festivities, but the proceedings were further enlivened by exploding charges of gunpowder inserted in granite boulders. Tony Deane and Tony Shaw in *The Folklore of Cornwall* say that in west Cornwall 'poles surmounted by sycamore bushes were set up on the highest points of every tin works, with flags hoisted from the engine houses'.

Readers may have noticed that in this account of Midsummer customs there are precious few references to agriculture. Country customs, yes; but specifically farming associations, no. Some had, in the course of time, become urban rather than rural affairs; others had women as their chief participants. All this is explained by the fact that June is the chief haymaking month, when peasants then and farmers now are preoccupied with getting their hay safely made and stacked before it can be ruined by the weather. As a country proverb of Devonshire shrewdly points out, 'Before St John's we pray for rain; after that we get it anyhow!'

One farming activity, however, which lent itself to communal operations and hence to certain celebrations when the task was ended was sheep-shearing. In Wales the sheep farmers of a district banded together to help each other with the shearing, all visiting each farm in turn. Their womenfolk went along to help with preparing food for the entire party, sheep were killed and dressed as necessary, and the occasion took the shape of a communal holiday, albeit a hard-working one.

In most English counties the shearing seems to have been done by travelling gangs, each consisting of up to a dozen men, who undertook the shearing of flocks on contract over a wide area. Each was under the leadership of a Captain, who worked out the itinerary and made the contracts with the farmers. My grandfather and my father were both at times, in the second half of the nineteenth century, members of shearing gangs in south Wiltshire and eastern Hampshire. My father has told me,

'We ate our meals where we worked and slept wherever we could, usually on a heap of straw in a barn. Our working hours were from four in the morning to eight in the evening. We rose at quarter-past three by the light of the stars and did four hours' work before breakfast . . . . Bread and cheese, onions and rashers, were our staple foods. We toasted the rashers on hedge-cut skewers over an open fire. . . . On my first night with the gang I had to sleep in a harness room. I spread a couple of sacks on the floor for a bed and laid my head on a brick, like Jacob, but it was not very comfortable. Also it was cold. In other places there were too many rats for my liking.'

Jacqueline Simpson has met men with similar memories in Sussex. She estimates that a shearing gang would shear anything up to 10,000 sheep in the three or four weeks of the season. She also describes the celebrations on 'Black Ram Night', when the shearing season ended and the final share-out of wages was made. This was evidently a convivial evening, punctuated by songs but chiefly notable for the quantities of beer consumed. My father's gang seems to have been a much more sober lot, probably because of a preponderance of chapel teetotallers. There was, however, some drunkenness, and he related stories of shearers who went down with delirium tremens and kept their barn-mates awake at night.

In *The Folklore of Hertfordshire* Doris Jones-Baker recounts reminiscences of oldtime sheep-shearing suppers, which had special significance in that county because it held the last overnight stops on the drovers' roads before London. Vast numbers of sheep en route for the London markets were accommodated and, if passing at the appropriate season, shorn. The suppers were evidently held in farmhouses and were more decorous affairs than some of the Sussex ones. The songs quoted for Hertfordshire are different from those for Sussex.

An agricultural reference relating to Midsummer which puzzles me is found in an account quoted by Brand in *Observations on Popular Antiquities* on certain candle auctions in Somerset. His story reads:

'In the parishes of Congresbury and Puxton are two large pieces of common land . . . which are divided into single acres, each bearing a peculiar and different mark cut in the turf, such as a horn, four oxen and a mare, two oxen and a mare, a pole-axe, cross, dung-fork, oven, duck's nest, hand-reel and hare's tail. On the Saturday before Old Midsummer several proprietors of estates in the parishes of Congresbury, Puxton and Week St Lawrence, or their tenants, assemble on the commons. A number of apples are previously prepared, marked in the same manner with the beforementioned acres, which are distributed by a young lad to each of the commoners from a bag or hat. At the close of the distribution each person repairs to his allotment, as his apple directs him, and takes possession for the ensuing year. An adjournment then takes place at the house of the overseer . . . where four acres, reserved for the purpose of paying expenses, are let by inch of candle, and the remainder of the day is spent in that sociability and hearty mirth so congenial to the soul of a Somersetshire yeoman.'

The practice of identifying an allotment by a totem would seem to be a good one for dealing with persons who, when the custom originated, were doubtless illiterate, but there are two facets of the affair which seem to me incongruous. The first and minor one is the question, where did they obtain, at Old Midsummer, apples large enough to take a carving or stamp of those rather complicated figures? At that season the new crop of apples is still small (they are not supposed to be large enough for use till after St Swithin's Day), while there are few if any varieties of the old crop which will keep till Midsummer. The second objection is that the tenancy of land from Midsummer to Midsummer does not seem to be a sound agricultural proposition. The letting of pastureland on annual tenancies is still a common one in Somerset but most of the auctions take place in April. This gives the new tenant a couple of months or so of grazing, followed by a hay cut and then more grazing in the autumn. A tenancy starting in the middle of the haymaking season does not seem logical, though haymaking is often late on the Somerset moors.

I am wondering whether there may have been a mistake about the date. Ruth Tongue, in *Somerset Folklore,* notes that the moors in question were enclosed in 1811, the custom probably ceasing then, so it would be nearly impossible to check. She provides the additional information that there were 24-acre strips and that the plots were measured with a special chain measuring 18 yards instead of the normal 22.

In some districts important fairs were held around Midsummer, some at least of them probably based on the need to disperse the first of the season's crop of lambs and calves. Cambridge still has a five-day fair around Midsummer in accordance with a charter granted by King John. A great fair was held at St Albans on 17 June, but that date also happens to be the feast-day of St Alban, patron of the town.

There remains to be mentioned one other agricultural, or rather horticultural, association of Midsummer. In west Somerset it is said that gooseberries are ripe on St John's Day.

*   *   *

A festival almost forgotten in these days when saints mean very little is that of St Barnabas, 11 June. An old rhyme,

> *Barnaby bright, Barnaby bright,*
> *The longest day and the shortest night,*

is a reminder that, before the change in the calendar in 1752, 11 June *was* the longest day of the year. The proximity of the Midsummer festivities perhaps accounts for records of decorations displayed on St Barnabas's Day. In particular, garlands are said to have been worn by choristers, clerks and even priests, and roses, lavender and woodruff are specifically mentioned in the composition of these posies. St Barnabas is often depicted carrying a hay-rake, as an acknowledgement of the fact that his Day marks the beginning of hay-making.

More than 400 years having passed since the Reformation, the Corpus Christi processions, still to be seen in so many countries on the Continent, have been largely forgotten. Corpus Christi was a great day in mediaeval England. The guilds paraded through the streets, carrying their banners and insignia, mystery and miracle plays were performed on temporary stages set up on waggons, and general conviviality was the order of the day. Corpus Christi refers to the presence of Christ in the Eucharist, a basic element of faith for all Catholics, and an essential feature of the processions was an elaborately decorated tableau in which the Host was carried, escorted by a large number of clergy, torch-bearers and civic dignitaries. It is a moveable feast, celebrated on the Thursday after Trinity Sunday.

CHAPTER 8

The Approach to Harvest

IN EARLY JULY we encounter further vestiges of the old Julian calendar, which governed our chronology until 1752. Under it 5 July was Old Midsummer Day, and local customs observed on that date or near it are under suspicion of having their origin before the change. One such was the Holne Revel, alternatively known as the Ram Feast.

Holne, a village on the edge of Dartmoor, has in a field a menhir, or standing stone, six or seven feet high, which was traditionally used as a slaughter stone. On 6 July a ram lamb was ceremonially killed there and its roasted flesh distributed to the people. According to one version, it was first chased over the moor and when caught was decorated with flowers, especially roses, before being slaughtered. It had to be roasted unskinned. Precisely at midday the carcase was cut into slices, and one version of the story says that young men would compete for the slices, to give to their girls.

The whole ritual has the scent of considerable antiquity.

Over the border in Cornwall Bodmin has an important festival a few days later. Here it has become associated with St Thomas à Becket's Day, 7 July, being held on the following Sunday and Monday, but the custom could well have originated before the time of Thomas à Becket and have been linked with Old Midsummer. It is known as the Bodmin Riding, though the meaning of 'riding' in this connection is obscure.

It was a drinking festival. Beer for the event was brewed in the previous October and was carried around the town in buckets, for sale to householders. One can appreciate that it was probably pretty strong stuff. The bearers of the buckets were several young men, elected as wardens for the occasion, who were escorted by a fife-and-drum band and the town crier. At each house the crier offered the toast: 'To the people of this house, a prosperous morning, long life, health and a merry Riding!' The band then played the Riding Tune, and the householder was invited to sample the brew and to take a bottle of it if he approved. Naturally, he had to pay for it.

On the Monday the Riding Games were held. They included, predictably, Cornish wrestling, as well as cudgel-fighting, foot-racing and numerous other sports. Prior to the opening of the Games a procession of horsemen rode to St Benet's Abbey nearby to collect two garlands of flowers on poles, which they bore to the sports field. A dance which started in the evening often went on all night. In the sixteenth century the Games were associated in some way with the local Guild of Shoemakers, but they had been established long before then. Recent attempts have been made to revive the Games.

In several parts of the country rural fairs were held on Old Midsummer Day. The one at Oswaldkirk, Yorkshire, had a Mock Mayor and Mayoress, who patrolled the streets in a cart, imposing fines for sundry alleged and ludicrous offences. The money thus collected, by two stewards in white aprons, was used to finance the games and festivities that occurred later in the day.

Fairlop Fair, in Hainault Forest, Essex, is reputed to have had a mundane origin. Many years ago a local landlord, named Dr Day, who used to collect his rents under a large oak, the Fairlop Oak, on this day, formed a habit of inviting his neighbours to a meal of beans and bacon under the tree before the rent audit. Other people came to see the feast, and sundry commercially-minded characters started to set up stalls to sell them knick-knacks and refreshments and to provide entertainment. So a fair developed by natural evolution. Perhaps. It could be an accurate account of what happened but it sounds suspiciously like an attempt to provide a rational explanation about something of which no-one was very sure.

Another event associated with St Thomas à Becket, being held on the Sunday after the saint's feast-day, was Lapford Revel, in Devon. Huge 'pestle pies' were made at local farmhouses to entertain friends who came to participate in the games. No dish was large enough for a pestle pie so it had a raised paste, kept oval in form by means of iron hoops. The pie contained a ham, a tongue, whole specimens of poultry and game, all previously prepared, seasoned and partly cooked. No details survive about the Revel, but it was followed by a fair on the Monday. The dedication of Lapford church is to St Thomas à Becket.

Late July and early August is a period when the interests of arable and sheep farmers tend to clash. Spring-born lambs are now fat and ready for market or rather, in the old days, for fairs, whereas the farmer whose main interest is in his cultivated land is preoccupied with first the hay harvest and then the corn harvest. In some years the two harvests ran into each other or even overlapped, but in others, perhaps most, there was a gap of several weeks, and it seems as though attempts were made to fit fairs into that gap. Certainly considerable numbers of them were held at that period.

Regarding fairs in general, William Cobbett, writing in the 1820s when they were being superseded by permanent shops in towns, had this to say in their favour:

> 'When fairs were frequent, shops were not needed; things could be manu-factured at home in an obscure hamlet with cheap house rent, good air and plenty of room, and then, by attending three or four or five or six fairs in the year, he sold the work of his hands, unloaded without a heavy expense attending the keeping of a shop. He could get more for ten shillings in a booth at a fair, or market, than he would get for ten pounds or twenty pounds in a shop. He could afford to sell the work of his hands for less, and thus a greater portion of his earnings remained with those who raised the food and clothing from the land.'

Cobbett's views on economics tended to be naive and entirely prejudiced, but it is interesting that today an increasing number of craftsmen settle in country cottages and choose as a window for their wares the local agricultural shows and similar events.

The attractive term 'revels', frequently used in Devon and other West Country shires was virtually identical with the northern word 'wakes'. A wake was a local feast-day, generally held on the feast-day of the saint to whom the parish church was dedicated, though in time the term was applied to a whole week when the factories of industrial towns were closed down for cleaning and repairs. The word itself has its origin in mediaeval times when a patronal festival was preceded by a watch, or wakeful night, in the church, in readiness to hear Mass at first light.

In compiling my book on *The Folklore of Wiltshire* I found a number of fairs traditionally held in the pre-harvest gap, several of them suspiciously near Old Midsummer. Stockton, in the Wylye valley, had a week-long feast which began on 6 July. There are references to roadside stalls for sweets, cakes, gingerbeer and other fairings, and 'five or six of the villagers got temporary licences for the week and sold beer from their own houses'.

Crockerton, near Warminster, had a revel on the Sunday after 7 July, St Thomas à Becket's Day. A local connection was claimed, it being said that Thomas 'used to come to Crockerton Revel dressed like a gentleman, and he would depart through the wood dressed like a beggar, in rags, having spent all his money at the Revel'! If it happened it must have been in the days of his youth.

In Hertfordshire the town of Hertford had a fair on Old Midsummer Eve, Ashwell one on Old Midsummer Day and Royston, which had a priory dedicated to St Thomas à Becket, a great cattle fair beginning on 7 July and lasting for three days. There were also fairs at Tewin on the 9th and Bennington on the 10th.

In Warwickshire the first Tuesday in July saw a fair at Shottery, and at Aston Cantlow on the second Sunday of the month. And so the tally could go on.

The last week of July saw another group of fairs concentrated around St James's Day (25 July). St James was, of course, a popular saint in the Middle Ages. A pilgrimage to his shrine at Compostello in north-western Spain was an alternative to the much longer and generally more hazardous journey to the Holy Land and during the mediaeval centuries must have been made by millions of people, who returned wearing the pilgrim's badge of the scallop shell. For those who were not able to make the pilgrimage a substitute was sometimes provided by constructing little grottoes of sea-shells and pebbles, where the devout might worship. London was one of the places where this custom lingered quite late. At Yarmouth and Brighton grottoes continued to be made, until late in the nineteenth century, on 5 August, which was St James's Day (old style). Children often made them to collect alms from passers-by.

Jacqueline Simpson *(The Folklore of Sussex)* gives an account of some interesting and apparently very old customs associated with the Horn Fair at the little village of Ebernoe on St James's Day. A cricket match is played against a neighbouring village, and while it is in progress a sheep is roasted. The head and horns are presented to the batsman who makes the highest score for the winning side. Ebernoe has a song associated with the Fair in which horns feature prominently. There would seem to be resemblances to the Horn Supper at Weyhill (which see p.137-138), and it is likely that we have here vestiges of some ancient ritual (probably none too respectable) the rest of which has long been forgotten.

St James's Day was also the start of the wheatear-catching season on the Sussex Downs. It is fascinating to reflect that these now rather rare birds were once, and not so long ago, numerous enough, albeit on migration, to have a recognised trapping season. But in Wiltshire, too, wheatears were quite plentiful on the chalk downs, both in the nesting and the migration seasons, until the downs were ploughed up during the Second World War. Miss Simpson records that the birds were snared in hair-springs set in T-shaped trenches, and I too was taught this technique by my father in the 1920s. Not that we ever practised it at that late date; he was simply introducing me to items of old lore with which he was familiar. But when he was a boy in the 1880s he often caught both wheatears and skylarks with horse-hair nooses.

The realization that St James's Day (old style) fell on 5 August brings us to the festivals of early August, the most notable of which was Lammas-tide. When the Government decided that the Spring and August Bank Holidays should be held on fixed dates some opposition and misgiving were generated concerning Whitsuntide but none about August Bank Holiday, it being generally supposed that this was not a religious festival. The idea was mistaken. The ancient feast of Lammas, held on 1 August, was certainly a church festival for many centuries, though it probably had even deeper origins.

Formerly two theories existed about the meaning of the term 'Lammas'. One held that it was derived from 'Lamb-Mass' and referred to the lambs presented to the church as 'Peter's Pence' on this day, which were dedicated to St Peter ad Vincula (St Peter-in-chains). Feasible though this explanation would be, it now seems fairly certain that the original term was 'Hlaf-masse' or 'Loaf Mass'. Lammas was indeed the festival of first fruits, which was based on the following passages from the Biblical Book of Deuteronomy (chapter 26):

'And it shall be, when thou are come in unto the land which the Lord thy God giveth thee for an inheritance and possessest it and dwellest therein; that thou shalt take of the first of all the fruit of the earth which thou shalt bring of thy land that the Lord thy God giveth thee, and shalt put it in a basket and shalt go unto the place which the Lord thy God shall choose to place his name there. And thou shalt go unto the priest that shall be in those days and say unto him,

"I profess this day unto the Lord thy God that I am come unto the country which the Lord sware unto our fathers for to give us."

And the priest shall take the basket out of thine hand and set it down before the altar of the Lord thy God. And thou shalt say,

". . . And now, behold, I have brought the firstfruits of the land, which thou, O Lord, hast given me."

And thou shalt set it before the Lord thy God, and worship the Lord thy God; and thou shalt rejoice in every good thing which the Lord thy God hath given thee . . .'

Taking this as a basis, our ancestors worked out a sequence whereby the first ripe corn of the harvest was cut, ground into flour and baked in small loaves. These were the loaves which were presented to the priest at the Festival of the First-fruits and hence gave the occasion the name, Lammas.

However, 1 August was, as we have noted earlier, one of the Celtic quarter-days, Lugnasad. 'Nasad' means a tribal assembly for the purpose of sports or games, while Lugh was an important Celtic god, who gave his name to a number of places in Celtic lands, notably Lyons (originally Lugdunum) and possibly London. Like Lammas, it seems to have been a festival to celebrate the beginning of harvest.

Memories of the old Lammas or Lugnasad customs lingered probably longest in the Scottish Highlands, where A. Carmichael, writing in *Carmina Gadelica* (1928-54), notes:

'The whole family repaired to the field dressed in their best attire to hail the God of the harvest. Laying his bonnet on the ground, the father of the family took up his sickle and, facing the sun, he cut a handful of corn. Putting the handful of corn three times sunwise round his head, the man raised the "Iolach Buana" reaping salutation. The whole family took up the strain and praised the God of the harvest who gave them corn and bread, food and flocks, wool and clothing, health and strength, and peace and plenty. When the reaping was finished the people had a trial called "cur nan corran", casting the sickles, and "deuchain chorran", the trial of hooks. This consisted, among other things, of throwing the sickles high up in the air and observing how they came down, how each struck the earth, and how it lay on the ground. From these observations the people augured who was to remain single and who was to be married and who was to be sick and who was to die before the next reaping came round.'

There are points of resemblance between the business with the sickles and the procedure at the end of harvest in certain southern counties of England. There are also affinities between the salutations to the God of harvest and the Harvest Home shouts once familiar in the south (as mentioned in the next chapter).

Manx folklore suggests that there were, in Celtic mythology, two gods of the harvest — an older god named Crom Dubh and the younger Lugh (apparently a sun-god) who forced Crom Dubh to yield the harvest from the dark earth. The story introduces an element of conflict and hence an occasion for rejoicing and celebration when the 'goodie' wins.

In *The Folklore of the Isle of Man* Margaret Killip records that by the middle of the present century all that remained of the Lammastide ritual was 'a general inclination to climb to the tops of mountains on the first Sunday in August and visit any wells that could be taken in on the way'. There was a tradition that in the old days the people who climbed to the top of Snaefell (highest peak of the island) behaved 'very rudely and indecently', and whatever happened certainly earned the disapproval of the Church. Miss Killip comments that 'it is said that a Methodist preacher put a stop to the hill-top rites far more effectively than the Church's prohibitions had ever done, by taking a collection at a religious service held at one of these assemblies on the top of Snaefell'. In the last phase, she says, 'the custom became little more than an outing to the hills on a fine Sunday in August to gather blaeberries'.

Lammas customs also lingered late in the northern isles of Orkney and Shetland. Ernest W. Marwick, in *The Folklore of Orkney and Shetland,* records that Kirkwall Lammas Market was once the great holiday of the year in Orkney. Here we apparently come across more echoes of the change in the calendar in 1752, for although this Lammas market was held on the approved date, 1 August, it lasted for 11 days, exactly the number of days 'lost' when the calendar change was effected. In Shetland fishermen held a feast on Old Lammas Day.

Kirkwall Lammas Market, says Marwick, used to attract people from every corner of the islands. To accommodate the visitors, the floors of empty houses were strewn with straw, — free lodging for those who did not mind sleeping with a crowd of strangers. Couples would agree to be 'sweethearts' for the period of the Fair, during which they behaved as married couples. They were known as 'Lammas brothers and sisters'. Folklore has recorded stories of fairy folk who visited Kirkwall Lammas Fair in disguise.

Lammas customs and memories are thinly dispersed in England, most of them being related to land tenures. In Westmorland farm rents were until, at any rate, early in the present century, payable on Candlemas and Lammas. And it was once evidently a widespread custom to throw open common pastures for grazing at Lammastide. In Wiltshire the water-meadows of the chalk valleys were grazed by sheep in spring; then the flocks were removed for a time to allow the grass to grow tall enough for cutting for hay; and after hay-making, which would naturally be about Lammastide, the meadows were opened for grazing again (though this time often by cows).

In Warwickshire Old Lammas Day seems to have been the stipulated date. Roy Palmer, in *The Folklore of Warwickshire,* quotes the customs relating to Coventry:

'Every year on the thirteenth of August it was the custom of the chamberlains, pinners and such of the freemen as cared to join them, all mounted on horse-back, to assert their rights by riding over the lands. Any gates or obstructions to free access were unceremoniously broken down.'

The riders were accompanied by a band, and the church bells were rung. The pinners, incidentally, were officers whose duty it was to impound stray cattle. This custom was last observed in 1858.

At Colchester and Staines, among other places, extensive commons were similarly restored to common grazing at Lammastide. At Staines in the 1880s a new owner fenced in the common lands, with the intention of abolishing the old rights, but a party of local people assembled at daybreak on Lammas Day and made short work of demolishing the obstructions.

Penetrating deep into history, it is possible to discover sinister associations for Lammastide. William Rufus, whose killing is held by some writers to have been an act of ritual sacrifice to the old gods, was shot in the New Forest on 2 August, the day after Lammas Day, in the year 1100.

Numerous fairs were held at this season, largely for the disposal of sheep and lambs, though in the course of time all the other appurtenances of country fairs naturally accrued. One of Wiltshire's biggest sheep fairs, which I often attended as a boy, was at Britford (near Salisbury) on 12 August, which is Lammas Day old style. In the same county 11 August saw a sheep fair at Warminster and 13 August one at Highworth; this up to late in the nineteenth century. Earlier, Trowbridge had a three-day fair from 5 August, while a widely popular fair was held on Tan Hill, All Cannings, near Devizes, on 6 August. Tan Hill was one of those ancient assemblies held on hill-tops, and the hill itself has attracted several stories of supernatural events. According to some writers it derives its name from a Celtic mythological person or god, Tana, who is in some way connected with fire. A more mundane explanation is that the name is a corruption of St Anne's Hill, the church of All Cannings being dedicated to St Anne, whose festival day is about this time.

The numbers of sheep changing hands at the Lammas-tide fairs were prodigious. In another book *(A Family and a Village)* I describe my father's impressions of the flocks converging on Britford for the fair, in the 1880s.

'We dodged through a maze of little streets in Salisbury, not much used as thoroughfares, but even here we had to be continually stopping at street corners to let other flocks pass. When we emerged into the wide highway of Exeter Street, alongside the mediaeval stone walls of The Close, the sight that met our eyes was almost uncanny. Before and behind us, as far as the eye could penetrate in that dimly-lit gloom, were sheep. Hundreds and thousands of them, in a bobbing, jostling, steaming multitude. They trotted steadily through the silent city, with only a glimmer of a gas-lit street lamp here and there to light their way, while the great, solemn spire of the cathedral loomed overhead, just perceptible against the dusky sky. It took us more than an hour and a half to traverse the mile or so between Salisbury and Britford. The entire length of the road was jam-packed with sheep, with intervals of only about ten yards between each flock. We reached the fair-ground just as the grey light of dawn was spreading across the eastern sky . . . .'

Cricklade, in north Wiltshire, had a Lammas Fair, held on the first Sunday after 12 August. It was connected with the opening of common lands for grazing rather than with the sale of sheep, it being the rule that every householder of the borough had the right to turn out nine cattle to graze on 114 acres of common land adjoining the Thames from Lammas to Candlemas. Miss Edith Olivier (in *Moonrakings)* says that the people of Cricklade had a reputation for being most boisterous and pugnacious, as the list of sports and games she records for Cricklade Fair serves to illustrate. It includes 'bull-baiting, hack-swording, boxing, wrestling, cock-fighting, break-heads (played with cudgels) and kick-legs — in which the opponents, standing opposite one another, kicked until they drew blood, the first one to do so being the winner'.

Devon, which still has a Lammas Fair at Exeter, had a curious old custom whereby farmers took four pieces of Lammas bread, made from the first corn threshed from the harvest, and crumbled them at the four corners of their big barn. The reason for the ritual is unknown.

Cornwall has a number of Lammas fairs and other festivities. On the Sunday after 12 August Marhamchurch has a 'revel', led by the Queen of the Revel, who is a local girl elected by the village children. Mounted on a white horse and accompanied by a band, she rides through the village at the head of a procession, mostly of children in fancy dress. The subsequent events include dancing around a maypole, gymnastics and, of course, wrestling (Cornish style). The occasion is said to commemorate St Marwenne, an obscure Cornish saint to whom Marhamchurch church is dedicated, and the Queen of the Revel has to lead her procession to a spot which is alleged to be the site of the saint's cell, but the date is interestingly near Old Lammas.

At Mitcham, in Surrey, a three-day fair was held from 12 to 14 August, in accordance with a charter granted by Elizabeth I. Norwich had on the first Monday of August a Rush Fair, at which large quantities of rushes, cut in the Broads and tied in bundles, were sold. York's Lammas Fair was traditionally held on Old Lammas Day; in fact, it lasted for 24 hours, from 3 p.m. on Old Lammas Day to 3 p.m. on the following day. It was one of the numerous fairs at which a court of pie powder was held. 'Pie powder' is derived from the French 'pieds poudreux', or 'dusty feet' and refers to a special court set up to try offenders, particularly vagrants and travelling showmen and pedlars, for offences committed during the period of the fair.

Some fairs of the first half of August have become associated with other saints, though they may have originally had connections with Lammas. This is especially likely in the Scottish Highlands, where harvest starts later than in southern districts and where the ritual described by A. Carmichael *(Carmina Gadelica)* would seem to be typical of a first-fruits ceremony. It is enacted on the feast day of St Mary the Great, which is 15 August.

'Early in the morning of this day the people go into their fields and pluck ears of corn, generally bere, to make the ''Moilean Moire''. These ears are laid on a rock exposed to the sun, to dry. When dry, they are husked in the hand, winnowed in a fan, ground in a quern, kneaded in a sheep's skin, and formed into a bannock, which is called ''Moilean Moire'' — ''the fatling of Mary''. The bannock is toasted before a fire of rowans or some other sacred wood. Then the husbandman breaks the bannock and gives a bit to his wife and to each of his children, in order according to their ages, and the family raise the ''Iolach Mhoire Mhathair'', ''the Paean of May Mother' . . . . While singing thus, the family walk sunwise round the fire, the father leading, the mother next, and the children following according to age. After going round the fire, the man puts the embers of the fagot-fire, with bits of old iron, into a pot, which he carries sunwise round the outside of his house, sometimes round his steadings and his fields, and his flocks gathered in for the purpose. He is followed without as within by his household, all singing the praise of Mary Mother the while. The scene is striking and picturesque, the family being arrayed in their brightest and singing their best.'

A little later in the month St Bartholomew's Day, 24 August, and St John's Day, 29 August, also attracted a number of fairs. A very important one was held on St Bartholomew's Day at Smithfield, from the twelfth century down to 1855. It seems to have been a typical pleasure and commercial fair but without any great emphasis on livestock and other agricultural commodities. On the other hand, Bampton Fair, in Oxfordshire, was noted for the large numbers of horses sold there, while Whittingham Fair, in Northumberland, did a great trade in cattle, sheep and cheese, among other things. In Cornwall St Bartholomew had, or has, a special role in Blessing the Mead, made by monks at Gulval, by Mount's Bay. He is, among other things, the patron saint of bee-keepers and honey-makers, and the blessing is given by an official with the resounding title of 'The Almoner of the Fraternity of St Bartholomew of the Craft or Mystery of Free Meadmakers of Great Britain and Ireland'.

West Witton, in Yorkshire, has a special festival on St Bartholomew's Day, he being the saint to which their church is dedicated. An effigy is made and carried around the village in procession, ultimately being taken to a bonfire, soaked in paraffin and burnt. The effigy is said to represent a character named Bartle, presumed to be identical with St Bartholomew, but no-one knows anything about him. One theory is that originally he was a local harvest god whose festival happened to coincide with that of the saint.

Carlisle and Newbury were two other towns with important fairs on St

Bartholomew's Day.

Our discussion of the fairs and festivals associated with the various saints' days of July and August has led us past the Day of one of the best-known of English saints, St Swithun. Even today innumerable people take note of the weather on St Swithun's Day, 15 July, and profess to see in it an indication of the weather for the next 40 days.

> *St Swithun's Day, if thou be fair,*
> *For forty days it will remain.*
> *St Swithun's Day, if thou bring rain,*
> *For forty days it will remain.*

A subsidiary belief is that apples are christened on St Swithun's Day. The boys in the Wiltshire village where I was brought up were confident that after a shower of rain on St Swithun's Day apples were fit to eat, a belief which was doubtless responsible for many a stomach-ache.

The popular explanation of the association of St Swithun with rain is that this kindly and humble man, who was Bishop of Winchester from 852 to 862, or thereabouts, requested that when he died he should be buried outside his cathedral, so that the rainwater from the eaves would fall on him and that the feet of the devout would walk over his grave on their way to church. This was done, but when the cathedral was rebuilt a hundred years later the monks of that time thought that the site of the grave was unworthy of so illustrious a man. They therefore determined to reinter his body inside the cathedral. On the date set for the translation, 15 July 971, rain started to fall, and for the next 40 days the countryside was lashed by violent storms. The popular conclusion was that St Swithun was angry that his wishes were being disregarded.

To rationalise the legend, it can be said that in most years, perhaps seven or eight out of ten, a period of rainy weather does set in, often lasting for several weeks, to the exasperation of farmers who want nothing more than sunshine to ripen and harvest their crops. The belief that apples are christened on St Swithun's Day is also based on sound observation, for they are certainly not fit to eat before then, whereas from about that time onwards the 'fallers' can be used for making tarts or jam. A Somerset saying comments that in June and early July 'apples go hidey', meaning that they are then difficult to see; thereafter they make rapid growth.

The probability of treacherous weather around the middle of July was also recognised in Shetland where 4 July (old style) or 15 July (new style) was known as Martin o' Balymus Day. Whatever the weather on that day, similar conditions would prevail for the next six weeks. Fishermen took special note of the tradition, putting out to sea confidently if the weather on the critical morning was fine. (Martin o' Balymas is said to be derived from 'St Martin le Bouillant', meaning the hot or summer feast of St Martin.)

In England the St Swithun tradition is known from Northumberland to Cornwall.

26 Rush-bearing in Ambleside, Westmorland

Certain pleasant customs unrelated to saints' days that were held in July were Cherry fairs or Merry Fairs. 'Merries' were a variety of large, sweet, juicy black cherries at one time grown extensively in southern counties, particularly Hampshire. The 'Merry Feasts' of Woodgreen, near Fordingbridge, were remembered when I was a boy. As the compilers of the Women's Institute publication, *It Happened in Hampshire,* record: 'People came from far and near to eat their fill. The days always ended in drinking and fighting, until a clergyman of the neighbourhood was so shocked at the proceedings that he bought up the "Merry Gardens" and stopped the "Sundays".' The trees were still flourishing in 1936/37, when the book was written.

A similar festival took place at Fawley, on the other side of the New Forest, and Chandler's Ford, near Winchester, had, until some time in the nineteenth century, a Merry Fair, while Odiham, near Basingstoke, had a Cherry Fair on 1 July. In Hertfordshire black cherries, of presumably the same variety, were known as 'mazzards'. There were many cherry and merry orchards in the county, and Frithsden, on the Chilterns, had its Cherry Fair. Warwickshire was another county with a tradition of festivals at cherry-picking time. The occasions were known as 'cherry wakes' and were held at certain places, including Shottery , Shipston, Stratford and Welford, until well into the present century.

Another seasonal festival of this period was rush-bearing. One is impressed by the genius of our ancestors in concocting festivals around the most utilitarian occasions, such as the laying of carpets, which is what rush-bearing, in effect, amounted to. Until the installation of wooden floors in churches and houses, which in many instances did not occur until the eighteenth or nineteenth centuries, floors of beaten earth or flagstones were covered with rushes, which were renewed once a year. The custom seems to have been observed with particular enthusiasm in the northern counties of England, where it often coincided with the Wakes weeks of the industrial towns. And, as already noted, in Norfolk great quantities of rushes were cut in the Broads and sold at Norwich Rush Fair on the first Monday in August.

In *The Folklore of the Welsh Border* Jacqueline Simpson notes that two villages of north Cheshire, Farndon and Lymm, continue the old custom, decking both church and graves with rushes on the second Sunday of July at Farndon, and on the second Monday of August at Lymm. The procession which bears the rushes to the church at Lymm is led by civic dignitaries and a Rose Queen and is accompanied by dancers. A short service is held in the church, and later refreshments and entertainment are provided in the village hall. Lymm used to have a rush cart, with a team of six grey horses to pull it.

Marjorie Rowling in *The Folklore of the Lake District* gives details of the long-established Rush-bearing at Grasmere, which is held on the Saturday nearest St Oswald's Day (5 August), St Oswald being the saint to whom Grasmere church is dedicated. The procession now has a religious flavour, being led by clergy and choir to the church, where a service is held. A hymn has been written, music composed and banners specially woven locally for the occasion. As a reminder of secular matters, however, a maypole is usually carried, and when the proceedings are over all who attend are given a square of gingerbread, made to a secret recipe and stamped with the image of St Oswald.

Ambleside, Great Musgrove and Warcop, all also in the Lake District, have similar rush-bearing ceremonies. Although the Ambleside festival is held on the Saturday nearest St Anne's Day (26 July), the gingerbreads distributed bear the Grasmere token of St Oswald. At Great Musgrove and Warcop the rushes are present only in token form, as in rush crosses, and most of the little girls carry garlands or crowns of flowers.

Rush-bearing ceremonies also survive at several other northern and midland villages, and, farther south, the Lord Mayor of Bristol annually attends a rush-bearing service at St Mary Redcliffe on Whit Sunday, when the Bishop of Bristol preaches the sermon. The rushes here are more or less incidental, for the custom owes its survival to the will of a prominent Bristol businessman of the fifteenth century, who left money to pay for the preaching of sermons on that day.

In a few places hay is substituted for rushes. One is Old Weston, in

27 Rush-bearing in Grasmere, Westmorland

Huntingdonshire, where a local lady bequeathed the revenue from a certain field for charitable purposes on condition that the field should also provide hay for strewing the church floor on festival day. Apparently it was the custom to wear one's new clothes on that day, and in her lifetime the lady had been considerably annoyed by the squeaking of new boots on the bare floor! The feast day in question in this instance was that of St Swithun.

CHAPTER 9

Harvest Home and Michaelmas

IN THE treatment of harvest and harvest home customs the writer must needs take account of the changed status of harvest in the pattern of human life, at least in the developed countries of the world.

When in the 1960s arrangements were being made for the daughter of a Los Angeles friend to visit England I remarked,

'What a pity she can't come in August. Then she would be able to help with the harvest.'

'I don't suppose she knows what a harvest is', said her father.

Now, for millions of people in Britain as well as on the other side of the Atlantic harvest seems sufficiently remote to be irrelevant. A wet week in August means nothing more than a spoilt holiday.

In the parish where I live it is still possible to trace, in more than one field, the mediaeval 'baulks' into which the open fields were divided. They are a series of parallel and rounded ridges a few yards across. Each baulk was, in the period when they were created, cultivated by a different peasant, for the general rule was that no peasant should have two adjoining plots, though he might hold a dozen or two in different parts of the parish. It is not difficult to imagine the bustling August scene of five or six hundred years ago, the fields alive with peasants, the men mowing with sickle or scythe, the women gathering the sheaves for tying, the children gleaning, or driving birds away, or looking after the tinier ones. Everyone was involved with the harvest, knowing that on it depended their living in the coming winter.

From such a scene to those of the 1920s or even the 1940s is only a short step. The harvest worker of 40 years ago would have recognised those mediaeval peasants, and they him. But between the 1930s and the 1970s gapes an immeasurable gulf. A peasant transported from, say, 1437 would find the farm of 1977 strange beyond belief. How could he reconcile himself to an economy in which the harvest is won by mechanics who make combine-harvesters and tractors in Coventry or Dagenham or some other urban complex which in his day were open fields? How would he recognise a harvest-field in which the only visible worker was a man on a giant combine? A countryside in which harvest was the concern of the few, the rest being merely spectators?

In the pre-mechanisation age there were no spectators. In view of the immense changes, it is not irrelevant to reminisce a little about the harvests of those days.

Of the inhabitants of the Wiltshire village where I was brought up in the 1920s all but a few got their living from the land. My father, who was then farming about 130 acres, employed four full-time men, plus a few pensioners whom he could call upon from time to time. But at harvest-time every farmer grabbed whoever he could. The able-bodied carpenters and bricklayers who worked for the local builder were roped in to help in the evenings. So were the shopkeeper, the blacksmith, the baker and a schoolmaster on holiday from the city. Pensioners, boys of ten upwards and women of all ages were in demand.

One of my earliest memories is of being trundled in a push-chair, with a can of hot tea between my little legs and a hamper of food sharing the seat, along rutted cart-tracks to the harvest-field, there to sit under the rick for a picnic tea with the harvesters.

'Go and turn them rooks off the sheaves over there by the hedge', my father would command, and away would toddle two or three tiny tots, who knew it was their duty to help. No spectators.

All the helpers were indeed necessary. To cart a field efficiently and without delays at bottlenecks, a team of nine was necessary. There would be either two or three waggons bringing in the sheaves, one being loaded in the field, one being unloaded at the rick, and one in transit. For the waggon in the field, two men were needed to pitch sheaves to the waggon and one to load them. Two on the load and three men pitching made for even faster work. At the rick, one man was needed for unloading the sheaves from the waggon; one in the 'pitch-hole', a ledge halfway up the rick; and a third passing the sheaves across the rick to the rick-maker. Four was the minimum, and five could be accommodated with advantage. And, ideally, two boys were needed, to drive the waggons to and fro between the field and the rick.

On an efficiently run farm the head carter would not be involved in the carting of sheaves until all the standing corn had been cut. He would be busy cutting another field with the binder. The sheaves which the binder threw out had to be retrieved and stood up in what in Wiltshire were known as 'hiles' but in many other counties as 'stooks', to dry. The more 'hilers' a farmer could recruit the better. This is where women, boys and old men could do their share.

So, at the height of harvest, a farm of average size could easily find work for 12 to 20 helpers. Every day's delay in a stormy season meant expensive losses. There was every incentive to finish the task as quickly as possible, and, even so, a harvest would usually last for from four to six weeks. What a sense of achievement, happiness and relief when at last it was won.

There was rivalry as to who would finish first. The word would go round that So-and-so had finished, and efforts would be redoubled. In oldtime Devon the harvesters would stand on the highest point of the farm and shout in triumph the news that for them harvest had ended. 'Arneck! arneck!' they shouted. 'We haven!' 'Arneck' was, I think, 'our nack', the nack being a bunch of stalks and ears of corn from which a corn dolly was fashioned.

The work of the harvest-field was carried on with precision. Under the tuition of an expert I myself became a passable rick-maker, though opportunities to practise the old craft are now non-existent. One started with a shock of sheaves in the middle of the marked-out site and, laying sheaf upon sheaf, always with their butt-ends outwards, worked out towards the perimeter. For every layer except the outermost each sheaf had to be laid with the knot of the tie on the upper side, but for the outermost layer the knots had to be underneath. The end of the butt of each sheaf had, of course, to fit on the bond of the sheaf below, thus 'binding it in'. The continual exhortation of the master rick-maker to the novice was to 'keep the middle full'. Neglect to observe this cardinal rule resulted in layers of sheaves slipping towards the outside. Props consisting of poles, hastily forced into position, were then needed to prevent the rick from collapsing and earned the ridicule of everyone who saw them. When the roof was reached the rule about the knots having to be underneath in the outermost layer was reversed. The centre of the rick was built up substantially, and the outermost layer was laid slanting down at an oblique angle, with the knots showing. The binding-in layer which held the outer sheaves in position gripped the ears only; and thus the roof gradually tapered to a peak. The tools for rick-making were two-grained prongs, short-handled for the men on the rick and long-handled for those pitching up. The rick-maker himself, except when working on the lower layers, generally used no prong but placed each sheaf in position by hand. When making the roof he worked on hands and knees, with often a knee-cap of leather to protect his trousers, like a thatcher.

The shape of ricks varied from region to region. In Wiltshire they were chunky and rectangular. In East Anglia they had straight sides but rounded ends. In Wales and certain western counties they were round. Scottish ricks were normally much smaller than English ones, this being because they were designed to hold no more than one day's threshing, a wise precaution in a wet climate and short winter days. In the late 1940s and early 1950s I started to compile a map of the distribution of the different types of ricks, but I was too late. The combine-harvester was too quickly making sheaves and ricks obsolete. But I did collect sufficient data to indicate that round ricks were chiefly predominant in the Celtic West, an observation which tallies well with the prevalence of curves rather than straight lines in Celtic art. A well-made rick would defy the weather for two or three months if necessary, while waiting for the thatcher to roof it in, though most ricks were thatched within a few weeks.

The binder (technically, the 'self-binder') came into common use towards the end of the nineteenth century. Before that, most of the grain harvest was cut by scythe. The work was undertaken in many districts by gangs of mowers who were led by a captain with the splendid title 'the Lord of the Harvest'. The scythes were fitted with an attachment of supple rods, known as a 'cradle', which, in the hands of an expert mower, threw out the corn-stalks in swathes as straight as they grew.

Behind each mower walked a boy, who 'locked' the stalks as they fell, meaning that he gathered them in bundles ready to be tied. Another child then extracted five or six stalks from each bundle and handed them to the 'tier', usually its mother, who tied the sheaves, twisting the stalks into a bond. If available, yet another child followed behind, raking up what was missed.

As harvest progressed and the fields were cleared of sheaves, the gleaners got to work. They were normally the wives of the farm workers, together with widows and children. Each gleaner, or 'leazer' as they were often known in southern counties, carried a 'lap-bag' of coarse sacking, which hung from her waist like an apron. Into this went loose ears that had broken from their stalks. Those still on the stalk were gathered with the right hand and passed to the left until no more could be held. They were then twisted into a curious little knot and deposited in a heap under the hedge, by the dinner-basket.

The right of gleaners to enter a field was an unwritten law, but it was also a rule that they should not be admitted till every sheaf was removed. However, the wives of carters and shepherds employed on the farm were exempted; they could glean between the 'hiles', if they wished. Only wheat was gleaned. Oat stubble was foraged by sheep; barley by pigs.

Gleaning was a necessary operation if a labourer's family was to survive the winter with any degree of comfort. An estimate given me of a season's gleaning, by a woman and two children, was from two to six bushels of good, clean wheat, according to the state of the harvest. When the work was finished, the surplus straw was snipped off, about three inches below the ears, and either used for littering the cottage pig or sold to a neighbour who possessed such an asset. The ears were stored in sacks in a bedroom. Later they were threshed by flail in a barn, the chaff being left behind to pay for the use of the building.

The grain was ground into flour at the local mill, the miller keeping the barn and milling offal as payment for his work. If a pig-keeping cottager chose to claim these coarser meals for his pig, he had to pay the miller a small fee. Millers had an unenviable reputation, though dating mostly from an earlier age. An old rhyme runs:

> *Miller, O miller, O dusty-poll!*
> *How many sacks of flour hast thou stole?*
> *In goes a bushel, out comes a peck;*
> *Hang old Miller-dee up by the neck!*

In mediaeval times a miller was permitted to keep only three hens and a cock! He was also prohibited from becoming a merchant, lest he should be tempted to trade in his customers' grain. He had to gain his livelihood from tolls.

With this background to rural life in the latter half of the nineteenth century in mind, it is easy to appreciate the importance attached to the harvest throughout history. It was indeed a matter of life or death. Mediaeval records abound in entries of famine. Examples:

'1041 . . . A year of storm and rain, with much consequent disease. This began a series of famine years which lasted till 1066.

1137 . . . A year of famine, with very poor harvest and corn excessively dear.

1258 . . . Owing to almost continuous rains, the harvest was very late, some of it not being gathered until November 1st. Many people in England died of famine this year.

1348 . . . An excessively wet summer, with almost continuous rain from mid-summer to Christmas. Serious floods followed, and much of the harvest was not gathered . . . .'

And 1348 was, of course, the year when the Black Death struck.

It is therefore easy to understand the rejoicing when, after weeks of unremitting

28 Harvest Home Supper in Sussex

labour by the whole community and the constant hazard of the weather, the harvest was at last safely gathered. Henry Alford's harvest hymn,

Come, ye thankful people, come,
Raise the song of harvest home:
All is safely gathered in,
Ere the winter storms begin . . .

now so often sung by congregations who have never set foot in a harvest field, expressed exactly the feelings of those who had been involved. That harvest home celebrations occur in the folklore of every county is not in the least surprising.

A central figure in oldtime harvest feasts was the Corn Dolly, or Kern Baby. Fashioned of straw stalks, traditionally taken from the last handfuls of corn cut, she represented the Corn Goddess, who gave the increase to the seed corn. It was thought that she resided in the cornfields, and her obvious importance entitled her to great respect. In some districts corridors of standing corn were left from one field or plot to the next, so that the goddess would have a way of retreat till the last strip of corn was reached. The reapers would then line up before it and throw their sickles at it, so that the goddess would never know whose hand had cut the last stalks. These were gathered up reverently and woven into the image of a goddess, which thenceforth held a place of honour at the harvest home feast and then by the family hearth. On Plough Monday (which see p.22-24) it was taken to the fields and interred in the first furrow, ready to work the necessary magic for the next harvest.

Although it seems probable that the corn dolly was fashioned into as near a likeness of the human figure as the craftsman could make her, numerous variations in design developed. Some were merely twisted columns of woven straw, with a topknot of wheat ears or with wheat ears suspended from the base. A specimen made for me in Essex in the mid-1960s is a beautifully-fashioned model of a lady in a long skirt, carrying a cornucopia as a basket. But recently such figures have become quite common, the art of straw-weaving having become fashionable again, largely through the auspices of the Women's Institutes.

In Wiltshire the custom of holding harvest home suppers on farms had died before my time, though old men whom I knew could remember them, which would put their demise back to some time in the second half of the nineteenth century. They remembered, too, the old Harvest Shout, which was raised when the last sheaf of corn was hoisted on a prong, preparatory to throwing it on the rick.

Well ploughed,
Well sowed,
Well harrowed,
Well mowed,
And all safely carted to the barn wi' nary a load throwed!
Hip-hip-hip-hooray!

The Devon version ran:

> *We-ha-neck! we-ha-neck!*
> *Well a-plowed! well a-sowed!*
> *We've reaped! And we've mowed!*
> *Hurrah! hurrah! hurrah!*
>
> *Well a-cut! well a-bound!*
> *Well a-zot upon the ground!*
> *We-ha-neck! we-ha-neck!*
> *Hurrah! hurrah! hurrah!*

The Devonshire hills used to resound to the shouts of labourers announcing the end of harvest in this way, like pheasants shouting challenges to one another. Mrs Bray, writing in about 1832, saw the 'nack', a stylised type of corn dolly, fashioned from some of the best ears of wheat and 'decorated with flowers, twisted in with the reed, which gives it a gay and fantastic appearance'. She describes how the whole company of reapers took this garland to the top of a hill, where one man held it aloft while the others gathered round and, brandishing their reap-hooks, raised the harvest shout. It was repeated three times, with a drink in between.

In Warwickshire one harvest shout was:

> *Up! up! up! a merry harvest home.*
> *We have sowed; we have mowed;*
> *We have carried our last load.*

An alternative was:

> *Hip! hip! hip! for the harvest home,*
> *Now we've taken the last load home.*
> *I ripped my shirt and I teared my skin*
> *To get my master's harvest in.*

They are recorded by Roy Palmer, in *The Folklore of Warwickshire,* who also recalls some of the songs sung at harvest home suppers there. One of them, used as a toast, was widely known throughout the southern and midland counties, and I have seen parts of it quoted on more than one piece of commemorative pottery, such as big cider mugs.

> *Let the wealthy and great*
> *Live in splendour and state;*
> *I envy them not, I declare it.*
> *I eat my own lamb,*
> *My own chicken and ham,*
> *I shear my own fleece, and I wear it.*
> *I have lawns; I have bowers;*
> *I have fruit; I have flowers;*

The lark is my morning alarmer.
So, jolly boys, now,
Here's God speed the plough;
Long life and success to the farmer!

In Warwickshire villages a horn was blown each morning or a church bell was rung to assemble women who wished to go gleaning. When all were present, the list of fields available was announced.

Mr Palmer records that the last load was fetched home with considerable ceremony, adorned in one village by leafy boughs and in another by bright ribbons and flowers, while the horses wore ribbons and rosettes, the driver was dressed in women's clothes, and the children, seated on top of the load, were in their best clothes. However, I feel that this could have happened only on favourable occasions, and not when the load was being brought in late in the evening or when a storm was threatening. 'When the last load reached the farm the mistress met the cart with cakes and ale.'

In Warwickshire, as in Wiltshire, the standard fare for the harvest home supper was 'boiled beef and carrots, plum pudding and ale, and bread baked in the shape of an ear of wheat', though more elaborate tables were sometimes provided. In the West Country, cider rather than ale was the usual beverage. Kingsley Palmer in *The Folklore of Somerset* records that 'at Tatworth a lady remembered how the waggon was stopped halfway through the gate of the barton and the men drank cider and blew on a horn'. This drink, of cider or ale, was known in oldtime Sussex as the 'Hollerin' Pot' — the 'hollerin' 'being the harvest shout and the 'pot' the pot of drink.

Jacqueline Simpson, mentioning this in *The Folklore of Sussex,* notes that the last load was generally a token load of just two layers of sheaves and that everybody who had been at all involved in the harvest clambered on the waggon. At Rottingdean this merry party used to parade around the village, calling at every public house in turn and raising the harvest shout at each. They finished up at the farm, where an 18-gallon barrel of beer awaited them.

Among the songs sung at Sussex harvest homes was one which I heard in Wiltshire in my youth, though connected with shearing rather than harvest gatherings. Evidently, though, it was popular at any festive occasion, as can be well appreciated. It was associated with the performance of the following ritual.

Each competitor was given a hat, generally a tall top-hat, with a flat top. He had to grasp the brim with both hands. A tall horn tumbler was placed on the flat top and filled with beer or cider by the chairman of the proceedings, who kept a large pailful of it at hand. The competitor had then to raise the tumbler to his lips and drain it without touching it with his hands. As he started to drink the company sang:

I've bin to Plymouth, and I've bin to Dover;
I've bin a-ramblin', the whole world over,
Over and over and over and over,

Drink up your liquor and turn your cup over,
Over and over and over and over.
The liquor's drink'd up and the cup is turned over.

The competitor had so to manage his drinking that he finished the draught while the company was singing,

Drink up your liquor and turn your cup over.

Still grasping the brim of the hat with both hands, he then had to jerk the tumbler into the air, reverse the hat, and catch the tumbler in it as it fell. If he didn't, the song was exultantly altered to,

The liquor's drink'd up but the cup baint turned over.

The unsuccessful candidate then had to go through the whole procedure again, with, of course, less chance of success. In some versions, the chairman had to have a drink every time a competitor did.

In East Anglia it was apparently the custom for the harvesters to collect money for the harvest home feast from anyone who happened to pass by the field where they were working. It was called 'Hollerin' Largesse'. George Ewart Evans, in *Ask the Fellows who Make the Hay*, says that it was still practised in Suffolk at the beginning of the nineteenth century:

'The reapers gathered in a ring, holding each other's hands and bending their heads to the centre. One of the party . . ., standing a few yards apart called out loudly three times: "Holla Lar! Holla Lar! Holla Larjees!" At the last long syllable he would lower his voice. Those in the ring would cry: "O.O.O.O.O." with a full, low note, at last throwing up their heads and shouting a loud "Aaah!"'

The man who collected the largesse would be the Lord of the Harvest, who also used to visit the tradesmen who did business with the farm and try to extract a contribution from them. Rabbits killed when the corn was cut were also sold to help the funds. In some of the poor harvests on small fields in Wiltshire when I was a boy the rabbits killed in the harvest-field were more valuable than the corn, but they were never sold but distributed by the farmer to the helpers.

In another of his books, *The Horse in the Furrows,* George Ewart Evans describes how in some instances the Lord of the Harvest not only controlled the mowing of the fields but also made the ricks himself. But in such circumstances the Lord was a regular employee of the farm, not a gang leader doing the work on contract. It was unusual, says Evans, for a stockman to be Lord, but a head horseman often was, and when he was working at the rick the second horseman had charge of the horses in the field.

The system of contract harvesting was, however, well known in East Anglia. The Lord of the Harvest would collect his gang well in advance of the harvest season and would negotiate prior contracts with the farmers, much as the contractor-owner of a combine-harvester now does. Enid Porter in *The Folklore of East*

Anglia equates the horn-blowing that went on in the early mornings with a kind of reveille to rouse the reapers. 'Any newcomers to a field were initiated by having the soles of their boots tapped with a stone by the Lord, who then demanded a shilling of each man to go towards the purchase of beer.'

From Harston, in Cambridgeshire, Miss Porter records a different version of the 'Turn-over' song:

> *We've ploughed and sowed,*
> *We've reaped and mowed,*
> *And we've gathered in all the clover,*
> *And every man will take his can*
> *And neatly toss it over.*
> *Now drink, boys, drink, and if you spill*
> *You shall have two, it is our master's will.*

Here all the company apparently performed together. It is said that the hats they wore were stiff straw ones.

Miss Porter also gives a version of the old rustic favourite, 'Green Grow the Rushes-O', as a popular harvest song.

In the eastern counties gleaning was not allowed to start till the harvest was finished and was then led by the Harvest Queen, a wife or girlfriend who had tied sheaves behind the Lord of the Harvest. She exercised considerable authority and made sure that all the women began and finished work at the same time.

The last load of corn was known in Norfolk and Suffolk as the Horkey Load, and the harvest home was the Horkey Supper. In Hertfordshire it was the Hockey Load and Hockey Supper, and here the harvest supper was followed by a day's holiday for the harvesters, known appropriately as the Drinking Day. It was for the beverages on that day that the Lord of the Harvest and his men collected largesse in this county.

The Hertfordshire harvest song was:

> *Master's got in his corn,*
> *Well mawn, well shorn,*
> *Ne'er heeled over, ne'er stuck fast,*
> *Harvest has come home.*

As in some other counties, the last load was only a token one and was carried through the village at a rattling pace. In a book of 1893, *Fragments of Two Centuries,* Alfred Kingston, writing of Royston and neighbourhood, describes the ensuing scene as 'Hockey Watering'. As the harvesters sped home, riding on the 'hockey waggon' and shouting 'Merry, merry Harvest Home!' 'from behind every wall, tree or gatepost along the route the men, women and even children, armed with such utensils as came ready to hand, sent after the flying rustics a shower of water which continually increased in volume as the hockey load neared the farmyard, where capacious buckets and pails brought up a climax of indescribable fun and merriment.'

In *The Folklore of Hertfordshire* Doris Jones-Baker notes that in one Hertfordshire parish a traditional dish consisted of huge rabbit-pies, made from rabbits shot in the cornfields at harvest. Gleaning here, as in East Anglia, was a post-harvest operation, extending over about three weeks. Gleaning bells were still being rung in no fewer than 20 Hertfordshire villages in the 1890s. Old records are quoted, too, to show that the regulations for gleaning were not always observed, the result being fights which became notorious in some places.

An alternative term for 'Crying the neck' in Hertfordshire was 'Crying the Mare', and the same term was known in Herefordshire, on the other side of the country. In Cheshire it was 'Cutting the Neck' and in Shropshire 'Cutting the Gander's Neck'. In *The Folklore of the Welsh Border* Jacqueline Simpson states that the 'mare' was the last sheaf. When the reapers lined up before the last strip of standing corn, as described above, they tied it into four bunches, which were said to be the four legs of the mare. The reapers threw their sickles at it, as described, but in some places, as a further precaution to preserve anonymity, they stood with their backs to the standing corn, which must have made the feat extremely difficult. Miss Simpson says that in these border counties considerable stress was laid on rivalry between farms in the race to finish harvest first.

It seems that here, a long time ago, the corn dollies and similar figures were plaited from the corn while it was still growing. At Herefordshire and Shropshire harvest home feasts the men fared rather better than in some southern counties where, as we have seen, they often had to make do with boiled beef and carrots. An entry in a diary of 1796 gives the following menu for a harvest feast: 'six chicken, three hares, two hams, beef, bacon, new cheese, tarts, plum puddings, custards, honey and ginger cakes.'

In Cornwall the old custom of Crying the Neck has been revived in recent years by the Old Cornwall Society. When cutting the last stalks of corn, the reapers here separated into three groups, who shouted the appropriate cries to each other. The harvest home feasts in the Land's End district were known, in the Cornish language, as 'gooldize', which means 'the feast of ricks'.

In the Isle of Man, where the ritual concerning the last stalks of corn and the fashioning of the corn dolly was observed until well into the nineteenth century, it is said that long after the old custom died one could hear of 'a last sheaf being quietly rescued from a binder and put away unobtrusively but safely in the barn'.

In *The Folklore of the Lake District* Marjorie Rowling states that in Cumberland the last sheaf to be bound was known as the 'luck sheaf'. An apple was tucked into it and the sheaf safely stored till Christmas morning, when the apple was given to the farmer's youngest daughter and the sheaf to the best dairy cow. The 'luck sheaf' was carried off the harvest-field by a girl, who later had the honour of dancing with the farmer at the harvest home feast.

The custom of making and keeping corn dollies is still preserved in the Highlands. In her book *The Folklore of the Scottish Highlands* Anne Ross mentions that she has been 'in farmhouses in central Perthshire where the Maiden occupies a prominent place in the kitchen, waiting for the first day of ploughing, when it is traditionally given to the horses. In this mechanised age, the cows often get the Corn Dolly instead.'

She states that the traditions and customs relating to the corn dolly and the harvest in general varied from district to district and from farm to farm, but that one of the most important considerations was who should cut the last stalks of corn. In some places it was the youngest person, boy or girl, in the field at the time, and to be chosen to do so was considered a great honour. In other places it was the farmer himself. When that happened, the farmer was, in some districts, entitled to throw the last sheaf into the field of a neighbour who had not finished harvest. He in turn passed his last sheaf to another neighbour who was still harvesting, and to be the last person to receive the sheaf was considered to be very unlucky. Throwing the sheaf in this way was held to be highly insulting and often resulted in violence if the recipient was able to catch the offender. In a good harvest the corn dolly was dressed as a young woman, but in a poor harvest as a hag, or *Cailleach*. So ominous and burdened with ill luck was the *Cailleach* that 'a crofter would seemingly prefer to see his best cow drop dead than to have the Cailleach thrown into his fields'.

The use of the last sheaf or the corn dolly fashioned from it as a sort of curse seems to be a deterioration from the reverence given it as the embodiment of the Corn Goddess. Ernest W. Marwick, in *The Folklore of Orkney and Shetland,* says that the figure made from the last standing corn in Orkney used to be a dog, or bitch. Formerly it was 'hoisted in a prominent position in the stackyard or on one of the farm buildings', but later it was used as an insult to the farmer last with his harvest. It might be tied to his cart-tail or set on his chimney.

Another Orkney custom was to prepare a bannock of flour, melted butter and fruit and offer it to the man who had brought the last load of sheaves into the stackyard. In the meantime he had had his trousers removed and his bottom scrubbed with the butt-end of a sheaf. As soon as he received the bannock he was given a good start and then had to run as fast as he could. If he could outdistance the rest of the men, who were in full cry after him, he was allowed to keep and eat the bannock. An alternative version was to require the man who brought the last load to shin to the top of the tallest rick in the yard, while his mates tried to prevent him. If he succeeded he was given a bannock and a bottle of ale.

In Orkney, too, 'harvest knots' or 'harvest roses', little emblems suitable for buttonholes, were fashioned from straw. Apparently girls and boys used to exchange them, but it was also held that if one of them could be placed in the toe of the farmer's boot without his knowledge he had to provide the harvesters with a bottle of whisky.

Ernest Marwick describes the meal given to the harvesters of Orkney and Shetland at the end of harvest as 'a simple little feast'.

Few if any harvest home suppers held in England today can claim an unbroken link with oldtime harvest feasts. From being a normal item in the rural calendar harvest homes became an optional event, staged or otherwise at the whim of individual farmers. The hard times which beset agriculture after American and

Canadian wheat began to be imported in the 1870s gradually caused them to be eliminated.

Since the Second World War there have been revivals. A few have been on individual farms but more have been communal efforts, in many instances organised by Young Farmers' Clubs. During the war on our Wiltshire farm we were helped with the harvest by groups of people who came to live for a few weeks in 'Harvest Camps'. Youth groups, scouts and guides, church organisations and others arranged the camps, pitching their tents under the big elms and spending a useful, enjoyable but decidedly arduous holiday. The harvest would culminate, after the last load was carted to the ricks, in an impromptu concert around a camp-fire, with barbecues going (although we did not then know the word 'barbecue'!). These occasions came very near to recapturing the spontaneous rejoicing of oldtime harvest feasts.

In, I think, 1947, when I was chairman of the Wiltshire Federation of Young Farmers' Clubs, we organised a village harvest home in my native village. This was a sit-down meal in the village hall, followed by speeches in which a farmer, a land-girl, a farm worker, an auxiliary from a harvest camp, a corn merchant, the vicar and one or two other speakers described what the harvest had meant to them. It made an interesting radio programme.

Recent harvest homes I have attended include (a) a Young Farmers' Club Harvest Home Supper, at which there was a guest speaker and a number of toasts, followed by a dance, (b) a Women's Institute Harvest Supper, followed by some musical items and a bingo session, and (c) a church harvest home, followed by an auction of produce, designed to raise money for church heating.

Church and charity harvest homes are now perhaps the most numerous of all harvest events. They seem a natural extension of the Harvest Festival services, which almost every church in the country now holds in September or October. In Wiltshire when I was a boy it was the custom for the chapel harvest festivals to be followed by an additional service on the Monday evening, with an auction of produce in the schoolroom at the conclusion. The Anglican church in the same parish used to send its harvest produce to the hospital, but one gathers that hospitals are now none too keen on garden produce which needs a lot of preparation for cooking. Very recently I attended a village Anglican harvest festival service after which the produce was sold by auction, in the church, on the Sunday evening, with tea, coffee and cakes served to those who stayed behind to bid. Some were doubtful about the propriety of the proceedings but enjoyed them nevertheless. It is worth recalling that church Harvest Thanksgiving services date from only 1843, when Rev. R.S. Hawker held the first one at his church at Morwenstow, in Cornwall.

*   *   *

The series of fairs which continues somewhat desultorily throughout the harvest period builds up to a climax at Michaelmas, which is a major landmark in the country year. Not only is it the season of great livestock sales but most farm tenancies run from Michaelmas to Michaelmas, and for a few weeks the advertisement pages of provincial newspapers are filled with notices of dispersal sales for farmers who are giving up farming. It is the season, too, when jobs are changed, and in the old days the Michaelmas fairs played an important role as a kind of forum where contracts were made between employers and employees. Modern Michaelmas is, of course, 29 September, but Michaelmas (old style) fell on 10 October, and some Michaelmas events still stick to the old date or thereabouts.

Among the fairs which were predominantly agricultural and especially planned for the dispersal of livestock were the great sheep fairs of the chalk downlands. One of the biggest, still flourishing, is Wilton Great Fair, held rather earlier than Michaelmas, the traditional date being 12 September. In the 1860s, at the height of agricultural prosperity, up to 100,000 sheep were sold there annually. Weyhill, near Andover, also had a huge fair of very ancient origin, for it occupied the same site from the eleventh down to the present century and was held on Old Michaelmas Day, 10 October. In the late eighteenth century, when sheep were fetching about 12 shillings each, it is said that £300,000 changed hands in sheep sales at this fair. Reputed to be even larger in its heyday was St Giles Fair, Winchester, which extended over 16 days around 12 September, during which period no business could be transacted within seven leagues of the hill on which it was held. It took the form, say old records, of a temporary city, whole streets of booths being erected, each for the sale of a particular commodity. The charter for this fair was granted by King William II, and the tolls went into the coffers of the Bishop of Winchester.

Many of the downland fairs of Wessex were held in places remote from towns and villages, particularly on hill-tops. Examples were Yarnbury Castle Fair (which was held within the ramparts of an Iron Age earthwork), Cold Berwick (on a hill near Hindon) and St Giles Fair itself, which was held on St Giles' Hill. A careful study of the sites reveals that, although they were far from centres of human population, they were well situated for the convenience of the sheep population, grazing on the chalk hills. Some of the hill-top earthworks seem never to have been permanently inhabited and may originally have been constructed partly as corrals for cattle and sheep on such communal occasions as shearing, branding and slaughtering. Their period of use may well have extended for over 2000 years, down to the later years of the nineteenth century. As for Weyhill Fair, that was said to have grown up on the spot where the Tin Road from Cornwall to London crossed the Gold Road from Ireland to Dover, though whether that is pure conjecture or founded on ancient traditions is not known.

Interesting customs are attached to some of these old fairs. At Wilton Great Fair the shepherds of Salisbury Plain used to assemble on the evening prior to the Fair and contend for the title 'King of the Shepherds'. It was not a contest of skill in shepherding but a straightforward fight, featuring cudgel-fighting, kicking, wrestling, and no holds barred. The battles over, the shepherds slept on the barn

floor in a circle, feet outwards and heads resting on their most valuable possession, their dogs.

A similar fight used to be staged regularly at Hurstbourne Priors, near Andover, where shepherds of Hampshire, Wiltshire and Somerset fought each other with cudgels (or 'shepherd's sticks'). Here certain basic rules were laid down; they might strike each other anywhere except on the face, and the contest ended when the first blood was drawn.

Weyhill Fair had its Horn Supper, where new shepherds were initiated in a Horning Ceremony. Each was made to stand with a metal cup, filled with ale and set between a pair of ram's horns, on his head while the company chanted the following verse:

> *Swift is the hare; cunning is the fox;*
> *Why should not this little calf grow up to be an ox!*
> *To get his own living among the briars and thorns,*
> *And die like his daddy, with a great pair of horns.*

29 Sheep Fair at Alresford, Hampshire, in the 1930s

That, I would think, is the oldest version, though there are others, notably one which ends,

> *And drink like his daddy, with a great pair of horns!*
> *Horns, boys! horns, boys! horns!*
> *And drink like his daddy with a great pair of horns!*

It transforms the verse into a mere drinking song, whereas 'die like his daddy' has a sinister ring of antiquity about it. Though, of course, a drinking song it was, for the initiate had first to drain the cup himself and then pay for a half-a-gallon of ale for drinks all around.

Sherborne Fair, held on the first Monday after 10 October, was known as Pack Monday Fair, possibly a reference to the packs of pedlars in mediaeval times, though a local tradition says it commemorates the occasion when workmen building the Abbey packed up work in order to go to the Fair. Formerly it was heralded by the ringing of a great bell in the early hours and by boys patrolling the streets and blowing cows' horns.

Nottingham Goose Fair formerly went on for 21 days, beginning on 2 October. Again there are two versions of how it derived its name. The local explanation was that it referred to the occasion when a farmer from the Forest brought his three grown-up sons to the Fair after keeping them in seclusion all their lives. They gazed in wonder at all they saw, presently noticing a group of girls arrayed in their fair-time finery. 'Aw, those are only silly geese', said their father, in reply to their eager enquiries. When, later, he asked them what they would like him to buy, to take home as a memento of the Fair, all three replied, 'Oh, father, buy me a goose!' The more mundane explanation is that the Fair was indeed noted for its geese, immense numbers of which were brought there to be sold, particularly from the Fens.

Geese, of course, are naturally associated with Michaelmas. It used to be a tradition in many parts of the country for geese to 'go a-stubbling', meaning to glean stray grains in the harvest-fields after the sheaves had been removed. By the time this exercise ended, around Michaelmas, the geese were in prime condition. Several Devonshire fairs, including those held at this season at Tavistock and Brent, were known as Goose Fairs. In Hertfordshire it was considered unlucky not to eat a 'stubble goose' at Michaelmas. Cornwall had a Roast Goose Fair on 12 October at Redruth, when the poorer people could expect to enjoy a meal, if not of roast goose at least of meat. Doris Jones-Baker, in *The Folklore of Hertfordshire*, says, 'It was traditional for tenants to send a present of a goose to their landlords at Michaelmas', and the same custom seems to have been prevalent in west Somerset, for R.W. Patten, in *Exmoor Custom and Song*, quotes an old song:

> *And when the tenants come to pay their quarters' rent,*
> *They bring some fowl at Michaelmas, a dish of fish at Lent,*
> *At Christmas a capon, at Michaelmas a goose,*
> *And something else at New Year's Eve for fear the lease fly loose.*

Many of the autumn fairs, especially in Devon, were known as Glove Fairs, because their opening was marked by the hoisting of a glove on a decorated pole. They were said to be held 'under the glove'. Certain midland fairs, examples being the Birmingham Michaelmas Fair and Baldock Fair, were termed Onion Fairs, or, in the case of Baldock, the Cheese and Onion Fair. Baldock was noted for its cheeses, while the onions displayed at both fairs came mostly from onion-growing districts in Buckinghamshire. A speciality sold at fairs at Bedford and Harpenden, among other places in that district, was a variety of pear known as the Warden pear. They were sold as 'hot baked wardens'. Hatfield Fair has given a word to the English language, for it was held on the day of the town's patron saint, St Etheldreda or Awdry, and the cheap fripperies sold there eventually produced the adjective 'tawdry'.

Although the distinction was later lost, there was a difference in origin between the commercial fairs, established by charter for the selling of agricultural and other fare, and the hiring or statute fairs, (known in some places as 'statty' or 'stattis' fairs). The latter were 'survivals of the statute sessions held to proclaim the rates of wages fixed under the Statutes of Labourers', enacted from the fourteenth century onwards. In many instances the statute fair merged with a convenient business and pleasure fair. Its dominant feature was the presence of workers, of both sexes, seeking employment for the coming year. Traditionally, they stood around wearing the emblems of their craft or trade, a tuft of wool or a crook for a shepherd, a whip for a carter, straw for a cowman, a mop for a maid. This last item supplied the alternative name of 'Mop Fairs', by which they were often known. Hiring fairs were once held in most English counties, though an investigator in Cornwall in 1913 could find no memories of them there.

Detailed accounts of some local hiring fairs are to be found in Roy Palmer's *The Folklore of Warwickshire*. He notes that when a person was engaged for the year he or she exchanged their emblem for ribbons. The new employer would present his employee with a shilling as 'earnest money', which the recipient would promptly go and spend on 'the fun of the fair'. He quotes an 1827 writer to the effect that the 'girls wishing to be hired were in a spot apart from the men and boys, and all stood not unlike cattle at a fair waiting for dealers . . . .' This was one of the aspects of the fairs which another writer in 1883, Francis Heath in *Peasant Life in the West of England*, fulminated against: 'Young girls dressed in their finest clothes were exhibited like cattle to be hired by the would-be employers, who came to the fair to seek their services, and the scenes which frequently took place at the close of the day were too disgraceful for description.'

Warwickshire had an additional custom which seems to be unknown in most other regions, the Runaway Mop. It was held a week or two after a local hiring fair and gave any who were dissatisfied with their bargain a chance to change.

In Devon certain hiring fairs, as those at Holsworthy, Okehampton and South Molton, were known as 'Giglet Fairs', though they were apparently associated with other seasons (Lady Day and Christmas) as well as Michaelmas. Canterbury hiring fair, on 10 October, was termed the 'Jack and Joan Fair', for obvious reasons.

In addition to fairs, Michaelmas was also associated with feasts or wakes and other festivities, and often all became merged with the local fair. Stratford Mop Fair is still a notable occasion. Formerly several oxen as well as pigs and sheep were roasted in the streets, and boisterous sports prevailed. At King's Norton Victorian rectitude was so offended that in the end its fair was suppressed. A writer in 1877 reported:

'Shouting hobbledehoys, screaming girls, drunken men and shouting women swarmed from the station in hundreds . . . . The public houses were packed, and customers had to fight their way in and out, treading on floors wet with slopped beer . . . . The general proceedings offered a spectacle of debauchery, drunkenness, noise and blasphemy.'

About the same time Birmingham Onion Fair was banished, in response to similar allegations, from the Bull Ring to a piece of land outside the city boundaries, where it failed to flourish. Many old fairs do survive, however, being kept going largely by travelling showmen, who trundle their roundabouts, switchbacks, shooting galleries, boxing booths, sweetmeats stalls and other attractions around a recognised circuit and are most assiduous in maintaining their ancient rights, often in the face of opposition from the local tradesmen and the police, who object to the dislocation of normal traffic.

Some of the reprehensible behaviour at fairs may have been due in part to the survival of an old belief that, for a short period, the law was in abeyance and could not exact retribution for offences. An echo of this belief was to be detected in Kidderminster's 'Lawless Hour', between 3 p.m. and 4 p.m. on Michaelmas Day, when the citizens threw apples, cabbage stalks and other missiles at each other and particularly at the town's dignitaries. It finally ceased in about 1845. In Lincolnshire and Yorkshire feasts were held on Michaelmas Eve, when for a short time the distinction between master and man was obliterated.

At Hertford and St Albans, Michaelmas, or some day in near proximity, was mayor-making day. The mayor was sworn in and presided at his inaugural feast. Poole, Folkestone, Nottingham and Hastings were other towns which installed their mayors at around this date. But again an element of ridicule of authority creeps in, as in Cornwall, where at Penryn and Lostwithiel a 'mock mayor' was elected and made merry with his drinking comrades. The Lostwithiel event was held on Old Michaelmas Day.

Some Michaelmas customs were associated with land tenure. At Wootton Bassett, in Wiltshire, the tenants of the lord of the manor met in secret to participate in a 'Word Ale', the purpose of which was to perpetuate an exemption from tithes which was originally granted by a Cistercian abbot in the twelfth century. Prayers were said, hymns were sung, and much ale consumed. At Rochford, in Essex, a somewhat similar ceremony was held, the conversations between the tenants and the steward being conducted in whispers. The event was held at cock-crow on the Wednesday after Michaelmas and was carried out by the light of torches. As each tenant was dealt with, his torch was extinguished. In this

30 Standing for Hire at Stratford Mop

31 Roasting the Ox at Stratford Mop

instance the purpose was not to secure exemption but to confirm what services were due.

In *The Folklore of Warwickshire* Roy Palmer states that candle auctions were formerly held at Warton, near Polesworth, to let the grazing rights on roadside verges, the bidding continuing till the candle guttered out. He also quotes a description of how 'somewhere about Michaelmas Day sundry farm waggons may be seen at intervals piled high with articles of domestic furniture with the rustic children seated upon the top. These are the belongings of the hired labourer, whose term of service being ended at one farm is removing to another.' That was a sight with which I too was familiar in my Wiltshire village in the 1920s. Certain cottages changed hands at most Michaelmasses. In several counties Michaelmas Day was known as 'Pack Rag Day' because of this custom.

At Berkhamsted no cutting of gorse or bracken was permitted on the Common until the first day of September. On the previous night the villagers interested in the right used to assemble and listen for the striking of midnight by the church clock. They would then proceed to mark out their claims. The gorse in particular was valued as a fuel for cottage bread-ovens. In Radnorshire poor people used to do the rounds of local farms between the two Michaelmasses, begging at each for a gallon of milk to make puddings and pancakes for a feast. Painswick, in Gloucestershire, observed a church clipping ceremony on the first Sunday after 19 September and on the same day used to bake meat or plum pies each of which contained the china figure of a dog. The origin of this latter curious custom is unknown. In another Gloucestershire village, Avening, the traditional fare for Holy Cross Day (14 September) was pig's head and apple dumplings.

Up to the early years of the nineteenth century the chief forester of Sherwood Forest had to give a report on the numbers and condition of deer there at a Swainmote at Mansfield around 24 September. At the feast which followed the traditional dishes included a boar's head, a peacock, ram's head broth and venison.

In the Scottish Highlands Michaelmas is celebrated more for the sake of St Michael than for calendar festivals associated with his day. St Michael is, in addition to being the triumphant champion of right against evil, the patron saint of the sea and also the escort who leads souls into the next world. Undoubtedly attributes of old pagan gods have been inherited by him.

On some of the Hebridean islands the inhabitants mounted on horses rode over sandy beaches. No harness but straw ropes for bridles was permitted, and seaweed was used as a whip. Both sexes participated, and races were run for small prizes. Anyone who had no horse was expected to steal one for the occasion. Other customs associated with the Feast of St Michael were the ritual slaughter of a lamb, the 'Michael Lamb', to be subsequently roasted and eaten, and the making of a special bannock. Carrots, for some reason, also played an important part. The subsequent night's festivities included several special dances and a type of mumming play, in which a woman falls dead and is restored to life by magic.

The Catholic festival of Holy Rood or Holy Cross, of considerable importance before the Reformation, has long ago been lost in England, and its date, 14 September, is so near Michaelmas that customs associated with the two have become merged, more especially since Holy Cross Day, by the Old Calendar, would fall on 25 September (new style). Certainly some of the big autumn fairs were traditionally linked with Holy Cross, none of them more important than Stourbridge Fair, at Cambridge. This great fair lasted for three days and was once reckoned to be the largest in all England, but it was in decline by the second half of the nineteenth century and was last held, I believe, in the 1930s.

Other events of this season were linked with the Nativity of the Virgin Mary, a Catholic feast-day which falls on 8 September (new style) but on 19 September (old style). Probably Barnstaple Fair, held on the Wednesday, Thursday and Friday before 20 September, was one of these. Both a commercial and pleasure fair, noted for its sales of cattle and horses, it was long the most important event of the year in north Devon. Among the ancillary events associated with it was a stag hunt on Exmoor, the stag being turned loose near Brendon on the second day of the fair. Woodbury Hill Fair, held within the ramparts of an old earthwork near Bere Regis, Dorset, was also associated anciently with the Nativity of the Virgin Mary.

Achieving wide publicity through Thomas Hardy's novel, *Far from the Madding Crowd,* Woodbury Hill Fair extended over several days. Roast pork and oysters were both said to come into season on Woodbury Hill Fair Day.

*   *   *

Michaelmas has naturally attracted its quota of weather lore. Fair weather on Michaelmas Day was considered to betoken a fine though cold winter, though a proverb current in Berkshire stated, 'A dark Michaelmas; a light Christmas.'

There were said to be three days in the middle of September (the actual dates being variable, though usually the 20th to the 22nd) which determined the weather for the next three months. If warm with a south wind, the next three months would experience similar weather; if wet and stormy, the next three months would be cloudy; but another version says that the three days should always be windy, and if they are not the ensuing winter will compensate for them by being unusually rough. In Cornwall, the critical date is 10 October, — Old Michaelmas.

In some districts the Feast of St Matthew, 21 September, was known as 'The Devil's Nutting Day'; in others, the epithet belonged to Holy Rood Day; but in yet others the taboo against gathering nuts applied to every Sunday. Most widespread of all beliefs is that the Devil spits on blackberries on a certain date in autumn, rendering them unfit to eat. Michaelmas Day is sometimes quoted, but that is probably through confusion with Old Michaelmas Day, for it is true that by about 10 October frost and maggot-producing flies have usually spoiled most of the blackberry crop.

CHAPTER 10

Hallowe'en and Bonfire Night

THE CELTIC festival of Samhain, which originally fell (before the change of the calendar) on 12 November but then automatically shifted to 1 November, was not only a quarter day but also the beginning of the Celtic New Year. It marked the end of harvest and the beginning of the gloomy reign of winter. The winter fires, which burned on the hearth all through the dark months, were kindled. Surplus animals were slaughtered and salted down for winter use. In far-off days a burnt sacrifice was offered to the gods. Samhain was also the day when spirits of the dead returned and wandered again upon the earth. Brands were plucked from the bonfires and carried around the settlement to chase them away before they could commit evil. Spells were cast, to learn what the future year had in store.

Almost all these aspects of Samhain, except the sacrifice, have survived in the customs and folklore attached to Hallowe'en, to All Saints' Day and also to 5 November, Guy Fawkes' Day, with the slaughter of cattle becoming associated with Martinmas (11 November, new style).

In the Wiltshire village of my boyhood Bonfire Night, 5 November, had inherited most of the old lore. We had a communal bonfire on the high hill that overlooks the village. We ran about with blazing besoms that had been dipped in tar. We made lanterns of hollowed-out mangolds or turnips, with grotesque faces and stumps of candle fixed inside. We burnt a 'guy' and enjoyed a firework display. And we boys were convinced that this was a Mischief Night, when none of our misdeeds could be punished. We knew the old rhyme,

Please to remember
The fifth of November,

Gunpowder treason and plot.
And I see no reason
Why gunpowder treason
Should ever be forgot.

But I cannot recall that we knew any spells or practised divination.

In parts of Somerset and Devon Hallowe'en is known as 'Punkie Night'. The celebrations today are centred on the village of Hinton St George, near Crewkerne, and some of the neighbouring ones, but they may once have been more widely spread, for R.W. Patten, in *Exmoor Custom and Song,* says that the 'punkies', which is the name given to the hollowed-out lanterns, are not uncommon in Exmoor villages. There is a suggestion that 'punkie' is derived from 'pumpkin', some of the lanterns being made from pumpkins, but I am inclined to the view that it is equivalent to 'bogey'. When we were small boys we used to prance down the road with the lighted lanterns under our coats, singing,

Moonlight, starlight,
Bogeys won't be out tonight,

and then suddenly flash the lanterns in the face of some smaller child, hoping to frighten it into believing that bogeys *were* out, after all!

Interestingly, the people of Hinton St George have evolved their own story to account for the Punkie Night festivities, which include a procession led by a Punkie King and Queen (children). It is said that the men of the village went to Chiselborough Fair (in a neighbouring village), got drunk and were late coming home. Their wives became worried, knowing that on their way home the men had to cross a ford, which may have been in flood, so they scooped lanterns from mangolds and then went around the village begging for candles and money to go in search of the wayfarers. That is why the children now on their rounds sing:

It's Punkie Night tonight.
It's Punkie Night tonight.
Gie us a candle; gie us a light,
For it's Punkie Night tonight.

The story is an interesting example of an attempt to give a rational explanation for an ancient custom the origin of which had been forgotten. It must be admitted, though, that parts of it are irrational, for it taxes the imagination to picture a lot of worried women taking the trouble to scoop out mangolds to make lanterns and then to go around the village asking for candles and money. What would they want money for, anyway, on a dark October night?

Chiselborough Fair, now defunct, was held on the last Thursday of October, conveniently near Hallowe'en.

In Scotland, where naturally old Celtic traditions have lingered long, it was a Highland custom to build the Samhain bonfire on a tumulus or barrow. Anne Ross, in *The Folklore of the Scottish Highlands,* gives an eyewitness account of the

Hallowe'en celebrations at Fortingall, Perthshire, which were last held on the traditional site in 1924. The bonfire was built, on the Mound of the Dead (a Bronze Age tumulus), by communal effort and was lit by the older men of the community. The people danced around it while it was blazing, and when it began to die down they seized brands from it and ran around with them. When only embers remained, the boys competed with each other in leaping across them. Then everyone went home and dipped for apples. In other places, the burning brands were carried around the boundaries of farmsteads, presumably to keep evil forces at bay. And the belief that this was a Mischief Night was widespread.

In the Shetlands, instead of carrying turnip-lanterns on Hallowe'en children used to put on fantastic masks and long white robes. They were called 'skeklers' and were evidently supposed to represent spirits or bogeys. One was dressed in black, as the Devil. Thus arrayed, the youngsters would make the rounds of the houses, asking for cakes or other gifts. Traditionally, 1 November (Hallowmas) was observed by a day-long fast, until the evening when each family held a feast, with a sheep as the main course.

Shetland also used to celebrate as Winter Sunday the third Sunday of October (old style). On the preceding day all the cattle that had spent the summer grazing on the hills were brought into buildings for the winter. In the Isle of Man the conventional date for this exercise was 12 November (Samhain), which was there known as Hollantide. (In Cornwall the name was Allantide.) An old Celtic festival held on Hollantide Eve in the Isle of Man is Hop Tu Naa, which are also the last words of a rhyme chanted by the children as they parade the villages, carrying turnip-lanterns and inviting contributions. It runs:

> *Jinny the squinny* [witch] *went over the house*
> *To get a stick to lather the mouse,*
> *Hop Tu Naa, Hop Tu Naa.*

In *The Folklore of the Welsh Border* Jacqueline Simpson notes that Hallowe'en parades by children bearing turnip-lanterns and often wearing masks, fancy dress or blackened faces are common in this area. Bonfires are also the rule, and 'the merrymaking often ended in a wild rush for home as the fire burnt down, for fear that a ghostly black sow would take the hindmost, since, so it was said, on this night there was "a little black sow with a ringed tail sitting on every stile".'

Here, too, the pre-Reformation custom of 'souling' lingered longer than in most places. Hallowe'en is the Eve of All Saints' Day, which is 1 November in the ecclesiastical calendar; and the next day, 2 November, is All Souls' Day. In Roman Catholic times prayers were offered on this day for the dead, and poor people used to collect alms in return for a promise to undertake the intercessions. The custom became ritualised, parties of men suitably dressed parading the streets and inviting alms by singing a 'Souling Song'. In Cheshire a Souling Play, which resembled in many respects the traditional mumming plays, was performed. A horse's head or skull, mounted on a pole and known as a 'hodening horse', played an important part in the proceedings. The performers were known as 'Soulcakers', the reference being to spiced buns or cakes which were given to the singers as they made their rounds. The term 'soul-cakes' later came to mean any gifts in kind or cash collected by the singers, and now it has been appropriated by children collecting money for fireworks for Bonfire Night! One old song, still in use recently, began:

> *Tonight we come a-souling, good nature to find,*
> *And we hope you'll remember it's soul-caking time.*

The words and music of the Soul-caking play and songs, as performed at Comberbach in Cheshire in 1926, are recorded in *A Country Parish* by A.W. Boyd (1950).

All Souls' Day customs, once widespread, became extinct in most districts in the nineteenth century, and interest in folklore was sufficiently developed to catch memories of them in their last, faded phases. *British Calendar Customs* (published in 1940), which includes a collection of such reminiscences, lists Staffordshire, Yorkshire, Northamptonshire, Derbyshire, Lincolnshire and Warwickshire, as well as the Welsh border counties, as shires in which at least some of the old customs survived into the nineteenth century. Most are concerned with children collecting 'soul-cakes' and singing traditional verses. In some districts the festival was known as 'Saumass', a corruption of 'Soul-mass', much as 'loaf-Mass' became changed to 'Lammas'. Specially-made bread for eating on that day was called 'Saumass loaves'. In Derbyshire and Lancashire All Souls' Day was particularly associated with bonfires, and in Derbyshire it was supposed that these were to light souls on their way out of purgatory, a conjecture curiously akin to the more ancient belief that on Hallowe'en the spirits of the dead roamed freely on the earth.

In Hertfordshire, too, children did their rounds, demanding soul-cakes, and Reginald Hine, who wrote a *History of Hitchin* in the 1920s, said that in a certain field on Hallowe'en men used to assemble at midnight, 'one of them burning a large fork of straw, whilst the rest knelt in a circle and prayed for the souls of their departed friends. The popular idea was that the dead were released for that one night from the pains of purgatory, but only so long as the straw continued to burn.' The field was appropriately known as Purgatory Field. Jacqueline Simpson records that in Sussex the custom of children 'going souling' on All Saints' Day died out only within living memory.

In the Lake District the belief in the souls of the dead being abroad on Hallowe'en was rationalised by the explanation that, this being the season when domestic animals were brought into buildings for the winter, the spirits of the departed could also expect to find a place in their old homes.

Although bonfires were originally only one feature of the Hallowtide festivities, they are the one which, transferred to Guy Fawkes' Night, has most widely survived. In probably every town and village in all Britain bonfires blaze and fireworks splinter the air, to the delight of children, on the evening of 5 November. The burning of the guy dates, of course, only from the seventeenth

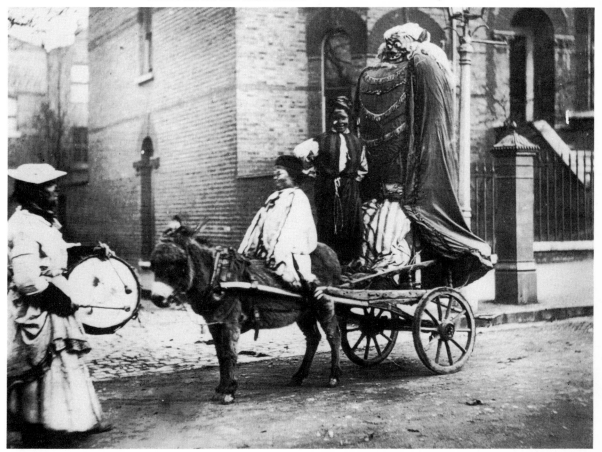

century, and, although the effigy is now almost universally identified as Guy Fawkes, in some places it was until quite recent times held to be the Pope. In strongly Protestant regions there was a distinct anti-Roman Catholic flavour to the 5 November festivities. At Lewes, which still has lively and extensive celebrations on that night, it was long remembered that 17 Protestant martyrs were burnt at the stake there in the reign of Mary I. In parts of Cambridgeshire the rhyme which begins 'Please to remember the fifth of November' has an additional stanza,

> *A rope, a rope, to hang the Pope,*
> *A piece of cheese to toast him,*
> *A barrel of beer to drink his health,*
> *And a right good fire to roast him.*

At Exeter a resurgence of anti-Popery sentiment occurred in 1850, when a well-organised procession on Guy Fawkes' Night demonstrated against both the Catholic Church and the Oxford Movement. But the Exeter Bonfire Night celebrations had by then become somewhat notorious. In my book, *The Folklore*

32 A Guy Fawkes effigy, 1877

of Devon, I remark: 'Things often got out of hand and flaming tar-barrels were kicked about the streets. At their height, in the middle of the nineteenth century, they used to last for nearly twenty-four hours, and people were woken up at four o'clock in the morning by the firing of cannon.'

Ottery St Mary was another Devonshire town with a reputation for lively Bonfire Night festivities, which are still held. Blazing tar-barrels are carried through the crowds, disintegrating into sparks and showers of melted tar as they progress. The custom is held to bring good luck. Efforts by the police and other authorities to suppress the Ottery and Exeter revels in the second half of the nineteenth century were met with enthusiastic opposition, a strong party of police sent one year from Exeter to deal with the Ottery crowds being tumbled out of their vehicle, which was then thrown in the river. Similar attempts to interfere with the old, boisterous customs in Lewes, Horsham and other Sussex towns were countered by the formation of a loose but effective opposition known as 'The Bonfire Boys'.

Elsewhere similar developments took place. In *The Folklore of the Welsh Border* Jacqueline Simpson quotes from *Folklore and Dialect of the Wye Valley,* by I. Waters, on the subject of oldtime carryings-on at Chepstow:

> 'In 1863 a fireball blazed on top of the Beauford Arms Assembly Room, and tar barrels were rolled down from Thomas Street, where a policeman was stoned and injured. The culprits were looked upon as heroes and defended by lawyers paid by means of a public subscription . . . . Year after year the magistrates tried to punish the trouble-makers, but were defeated by mass perjury and the shortage of policemen. Mobs threw mud and stones, kicked one constable's door in, and soaked another in paraffin and tried to burn him. Even the *Advertiser,* which had condemned the custom in 1855, declared in 1882 that it would be better if the police kept the streets clear on Sundays instead of "battering the heads of people indiscriminately on Guy Fawkes' Day".'

Again there is the emphasis on Guy Fawkes' Night being a 'Mischief Night', when offences might be committed with impunity. Usually any injuries which occurred in recent times were accidental, but formerly they were sometimes deliberate, for Jacqueline Simpson records that in the 1860s and 1870s at Rye 'it was quite common for people to catch those they had a grudge against and tar and feather them, to the great amusement of the crowd'.

Incidentally, the fireball mentioned above was probably made of 'old rags covered with pitch' and set alight. In many accounts of Bonfire Night celebrations gunpowder is mentioned, and doubtless it was widely used, producing dangerous but highly satisfying explosions. In Wiltshire in the 1920s and 1930s we used to put carbide in tins, starting it 'working' by spitting on it and then fastening the lid and throwing the tin on the fire. The results were quite dramatic.

Hallowe'en is, of course, kept up wholeheartedly in many parts of the United States. Masked balls and coloured lanterns, with 'bogey' faces, are important features of the festivities. Because Guy Fawkes is of little significance on the other side of the Atlantic, the old customs are observed on the proper day instead of being switched to 5 November. Many Americans serve pumpkin pie on this occasion, a dish too sweet for most English palates, though pumpkin pie was also a tradition at the 5 November Walkern Fair, in Hertfordshire.

In Canada, children, carrying little pails and often lanterns, knock at doors on Hallowe'en, inviting 'tuck and treat'. Recently a small grandson in British Columbia, by circling a couple of blocks with his bucket, collected enough sweets ('candies' to him) to last him the best part of a week.

I have some notes on an old Irish custom whereby villagers went around begging for cakes, cheese, eggs, money and other ingredients for a Hallowe'en feast, while their wives were preparing griddle-cakes and candles. 'The candles were taken from house to house, ready for lighting up on the next day.' There are obvious affinities here to the Punkie Night celebrations at Hinton St George, Somerset.

Divination, an important feature of Samhain festivities, long continued to be associated with Hallowe'en. Many of the old rites are concerned with apples, appropriately because by Hallowe'en the apple harvest should have just ended and apples are therefore at their most plentiful. One of the most widely practised rites was, or is, apple-bobbing, now usually performed as a game (in Wiltshire we often played it at Christmas) but formerly with a divinatory significance. The players have to take bites at apples while their hands are tied behind their backs. In some versions, the apples float in a pan of water; in others they are suspended on strings; in some they are fastened to one end of a pivoted stick, with a lighted candle at the other. Sometimes the apples are suspended by a thread over a fire, and the girls who have placed them there seek to determine, by the order in which they fall into the fire, the order in which they will get married.

Another common apple rite is to peel an apple in one long strand and throw the peel over the left shoulder. When it struck the floor it would form the initial of the peeler's future husband or wife. In Cornwall an old custom was to place a large apple under the pillow when retiring to bed, ready for eating first thing in the morning. Dreams would then be of one's sweetheart. At Hallowe'en fruiterers used to advertise suitable apples as 'Allan apples' — 'Allan' being derived from 'Hallowe'en'.

Nuts, also plentiful at this season, were likewise used in divination, so extensively that in some parts of the country Hallowe'en was once known as 'Nutcrack Night'. A common practice was to put two nuts, one representing a girl and the other her sweetheart, on the fire and to note whether they exploded or burned quietly. The interpretation, however, varied from district to district, some maintaining that the bursting of the nuts was propitious, and others the contrary. In some parts of the country (Suffolk, for instance), apple pips were used instead of nuts.

In the Isle of Man and the Lake District faith was placed in the making of 'Dumb Cake', which got its name through having to be made in complete silence. In the Isle of Man it was a communal operation, in which numerous girls assisted, and the cake was, after baking, divided between them. Each had to eat her portion, still without speaking, and then retire to bed, walking backwards. She would then dream of her future husband. Considerable fortitude was needed, for the cake contained, besides flour and eggs, the less pleasant ingredients of soot, salt and eggshells. In the Lake District the girl who prepared the cake placed it on the griddle and then went to bed while it was baking. Her future husband was supposed, in her dreams, to come and turn the cake. The Isle of Man also had another version in which the divinatory object was a salt herring, which had to be stolen. The future husband would appear in a dream and offer his understandably very thirsty sweetheart a drink of water.

A remarkable range of objects was employed in attempts to peer into the future. Cabbages would seem to be an unlikely medium, but in Herefordshire a girl could expect to see a vision of her future husband if she went into the garden and cut a cabbage as the clock struck midnight on Hallowe'en. Or, alternatively, she could pick a twig of yew from a churchyard which she had never before visited and sleep with it under her pillow. In Shropshire and Staffordshire she had to pick, again at the enchanted hour of midnight, nine sage leaves, one on each stroke of the clock up to nine. The vision of her future husband would then present itself. Another widespread belief was concerned with the sowing of hemp seed, which, however, could also be practised at other seasons and has already been described (see page 102). An alternative to divining by means of apple peelings was to confine snails in a box overnight. In the morning their slimy tracks would reveal the initials of the future husband of the girl who shut them in.

British Calendar Customs tells of six Market Drayton girls who sat up till midnight one Hallowe'en, each with a shift hung over the back of a chair in front of the fire. At midnight they repeated a charm which lasted for exactly ten minutes. The girl whose shift moved first after the chant ended was the one who would marry first. The same volume quotes a writer who, at some time between 1815 and 1849, travelling late on Hallowe'en on the Raynham estate, Norfolk, saw five men sitting in a circle in a barn lit by a lantern. In the centre was a pitchfork on which was hoisted a clean white shirt. If they sat in complete silence till midnight they believed that, if any of them had a faithful sweetheart, she would come and take the shirt. But no-one came, so they sadly concluded that none of them was lucky enough to have a true sweetheart.

Although consulting the future for true sweethearts and future husbands was the most popular of Hallowe'en divinations, seeking for omens of death was also practised. The custom of watching in church porches at midnight, more frequently associated with other seasons, was also observed at Hallowe'en in some districts. Some said that the spirits of those who were to die paraded around the churchyard on that night; others that the Devil read out the list.

In Derbyshire it was believed that a woman who was born at midnight on Hallowe'en had the gift of second sight, especially as far as her own family was concerned.

The period between Michaelmas and Christmas is naturally dominated by Hallowe'en and Guy Fawkes' Night, but certain saints' days in October and November are worth mentioning.

St Luke's Day, 18 October, has its associations with weather lore in the term 'St Luke's Little Summer', which refers to a spell of fine, sunny weather that often occurs around that time. In some parts of the country the belief is applied to Martinmas, the period being then known as 'St Martin's Little Summer', but it is less appropriate, 11 November being rather late. St Luke's was also said to be a lucky day for choosing a husband, and sundry divinations, applied also to other seasons, were practised by girls. Several important fairs were held on St Luke's Day, and in the west midlands bell-ringing at curfew time seems to have been a widespread ancient custom. In York St Luke's was 'Whip-dog Day' until the early years of the nineteenth century. Children in gangs armed themselves with little whips and chased any dogs found in the streets.

St Crispin's Day, 25 October, is, of course, memorable as being the date of the Battle of Agincourt, 1415, a victory which was widely celebrated on that day for several centuries afterwards. The custom lingered longest in places with local associations with the battle, as in several Sussex villages which had families with claims that certain of their members fought there. At Slaugham, Cuckfield and Hurstpierpoint St Crispin's Day was celebrated with bonfires and fireworks until quite late in the nineteenth century.

St Crispin, who was a shoemaker who suffered martyrdom in the reign of Diocletian, was the patron saint of shoemakers. Their guild, 'the gentlemen of the wax', long observed his feast-day, which assured them of a holiday and a convivial time. It was held to be extremely unlucky not to keep up the celebrations, and a Herefordshire rhyme runs:

> *The twenty-fifth of October,*
> *Cursed be the cobbler*
> *Who goes to bed sober!*

At Horsham the people used to make an effigy of some unpopular local person, to be known as 'The Crispin'. It was hanged to an inn signpost or some other prominent projection and subjected to ridicule until 5 November, when it was burnt. A nineteenth-century eyewitness remembered seeing the effigies of a man and woman thus treated. It was alleged that they had beaten a small lad (the man's son and the woman's stepson) with nettles and practised other cruelties on him.

St Martin's Day, 11 November, was a traditional date for the rounding-up and slaughtering of surplus livestock before settling down for the winter, though, as we have seen, in northern districts the holocaust occurred earlier in autumn. It was also a date upon which various rents and other payments became due, and some of the statute fairs, at which contracts for the ensuing year were made between masters and employees, were held on St Martin's Day. A few of the old customs survive. At Knightlow Hill, in Warwickshire, representatives of the villages in Knightlow Hundred still assemble before dawn to pay their dues to the steward of the Duke of Buccleuch. The payment is known as Wroth Silver and is, according to some accounts, in lieu of military service in ancient times, or, according to others, to maintain the right to drive cattle across a local heath. An interesting detail is that a forfeit for non-payment is 'a white bull with red ears', a coloration associated with magic and fairies, as well as being today represented by certain small herds of the old wild white cattle of Britain.

23 November is the Day of St Clement, the patron saint of blacksmiths, whose festival was observed in several parts of the country till quite recent times. At Twyford, in Hampshire, a feast was held at the Bugle Inn on the evening of that day, when one of the smiths read from the Bible the account of the building of Solomon's temple. This was followed by 'Firing the Anvil', in which ceremony a hole in the anvil was filled with gunpowder and exploded by means of a fuse. Sometimes an effigy of St Clement was made and carried around the village, with the aim of collecting money to help pay for the feast. Similar parades, for a similar purpose, were apparently once the custom in Sussex and Kent. The effigy was known as 'Old Clem', and the custom of collecting alms as 'clementing'. Firing the anvil was said to produce a terrific explosion, which sometimes lifted the anvil into the air and could be heard a mile off.

In the Midlands the practice of 'clementing' appears to have been widespread, and several verses which the children used to sing have been preserved. There, however, the association with blacksmiths seems to have been lost, and the custom merely provided an excuse for apples, pears or 'if you've got no apples, money will do'. At Lambourn, in Berkshire, special spiced cakes, known as Clementing Cakes, were sold at the Clementide sheep fair held there on St Clement's Day (old style), which was 4 December.

Two days after St Clement's, St Catherine's Day, 25 November, was also observed in some districts. St Catherine was the patron saint of lace-makers and spinsters (in the proper sense of the word) and so was popular in lace-making districts, such as Hertfordshire. Here children had a holiday on the saint's day, and family gatherings were held, when special cakes, known as 'Kattern cakes' were eaten. At lace-making schools in the county, at which other lessons besides lace-making were taught, the day was celebrated by a dance around a giant candlestick which stood in the centre of the room where the young lace-makers worked in winter. Similar celebrations were the custom in parts of Buckinghamshire and Northamptonshire, while elsewhere in the midlands St Catherine became linked with St Clement in an excuse for asking the neighbours for alms.

In many places, however, the lace-making festivities were associated with St Andrew's Day, 30 November, rather than with St Catherine's. Some of the old Hallowe'en customs, notably the regarding of the occasion as a Mischief Night, seem to have rubbed off on St Andrew's festivities in Northamptonshire. Here again special cakes or buns were made for the occasion. At Leighton Buzzard, in Bedfordshire, they were known as 'Tandry Wigs' or 'St Andrew's buns'.

In London 9 November is Lord Mayor's Day, and several other places, scattered throughout the kingdom, elected 'mock mayors' on that day. One was Bideford, which used to elect a 'Mayor of Shamickshire', who, with his 'wife', was carried around to the town's public houses, at which he made a series of speeches until he was no longer capable. There was a good deal of horse-play, with blazing tar barrels a feature of the occasion. Newbury and Randwick (Gloucestershire) were other places which once had a mock mayor, chosen on and for this day.

Several of the October and November feast-days are associated with weather lore. One old saw, doubtless no longer current, asserts that the Day of Saints Simon and Jude, 28 October, is always wet. Another is to the effect that the wind for the next three months will blow from the same quarter as on Hallowe'en, but another version associated this with Martinmas. Some county folklorists quote:

> *Ice on Martinmas to bear a duck,*
> *Then look for a winter of mire and muck:*

but the version I have heard more commonly applies to the entire month of November:

> *Ice in November to bear a duck,*
> *Nothing after but slush and muck.*

CHAPTER 11

Christmas and the Year's End

THE CIRCLING YEAR brings us to the crucial date of the winter solstice, the point where the tide of daylight is at its lowest ebb. Now, to the intense relief of primeval watchers, the sun stops receding and begins its northward march again towards the zenith. Some early religious ceremonies were designed to ensure, by magic and sacrifice, that this should happen. Another factor in the continued popularity of the midwinter celebrations throughout the centuries has been that at this season of the year a rural community has plenty of spare time and needs some sort of festival to cheer it up. As noted in an earlier chapter, there is little to be done apart from milking the cows and feeding them and other livestock. The plough and other implements of cultivation can safely be put away for several weeks.

Christmas, New Year's Day and the other holidays of the period are basically the same festival, that of the winter solstice. Even St Nicholas's Day, 6 December, has been drawn in, St Nicholas being, of course, identical with Santa Claus. On the far side of Christmas the situation becomes confused owing to the change in the calendar, as described on page 12. Christmas Day (old style) would fall on the present 6 January, which is now the Feast of the Epiphany. Some of the old Christmas customs are still attached to that date or, more particularly, to the Eve of the Feast, which is Twelfth Night (see pages 18-24).

Features of the Christmas festivities that are almost universally observed are the giving of presents, the decoration of houses, churches and shops, the singing of carols and the family feast. Others, such as the burning of the Yule log, are almost forgotten. The wassail bowl is a thing of the past, but the custom of wassailing the apple trees is still observed in a few Somerset parishes (see Chapter 2). Mumming plays have managed to survive in quite a number of places and are now becoming popular again.

The mumming plays are probably the oldest surviving feature of the Christmas festivities and put all the rest into a proper perspective. They present, in dramatic form, the contest between the powers of light and of darkness. The basic plot is always the same, but the details are often blurred.

In most instances, the plays were never written down until very recent times. Players learned their lines from their elders, who had in turn learned them from their fathers and grandfathers. Each one had to repeat exactly what he had been told, whether the words seemed to make sense or not. Often, however, his hearing or memory were at fault. Thus, in some versions of the play occurs a character known as 'The Ball Roomer'. Almost certainly he was originally 'The Bold Roamer'. In many of the plays the powers of darkness are represented by 'The Turkish Knight' (sometimes by two Turkish knights). The identification of the villain with the national enemy, the Saracens or the Turks, probably dates from the time of the Crusades. But in several versions the 'Turkish Knight' has become the 'Turkey Snipe', obviously through someone mishearing the words.

The hero is almost always St George. His association with England again dates from the Crusades. But in many versions he has become King George, a change which must have occurred after the Georges came to the British throne. Occasionally the hero bears what was perhaps his earlier name of Bold Slasher or Bold Soldier.

The other chief character in the play is the Doctor, with his Opliss Popliss Drops or Golden False Drops. He is the primitive medicine-man with his magic potions.

The Turkish Knights, or whoever represent the powers of darkness, fight with the hero and give him a mortal wound. As he lies dying, a frantic call goes up for the Doctor, who comes in and heals the expiring hero with his magic medicine. The dark figures steal away, and the hero rises renewed and triumphant. In some versions the plot has become so confused that it is difficult to tell which are the 'goodies' and which the 'baddies'. But always somebody is brought back to life from apparently certain death.

Two other characters appear in most versions of the mumming play. One is Father Christmas, who seems to be a recent introduction. He does little more than act as a compère, to summon the characters to the stage at the appropriate time. The other is a character usually known as Little Johnny Jack. He is a rather pathetic figure, hung with ten or a dozen cloth dolls, who represent his numerous children.

Little Johnny Jack is important, for he explains how the mumming plays have managed to survive. He is unashamedly a beggar. Entering towards the end of the play, he recites a verse such as:

> In comes I, Little Johnny Jack,
> With my wife and my family on my back.
> My family's large, and my wife is small,

And I am the father of them all.
Roast beef, plum pudding and mince pie,
Who likes them better than Father Christmas and I?
Nobody.
A jug of Christmas ale, sir, will make our voices ring.
Money in our pockets is a very good thing.
So, ladies and gentlemen, be at your ease,
And give us poor Mummers just what you please.

The speech reveals the mumming plays for what they became — a means by which the poor obtained Christmas charity from the rich. It was the custom for village mummers to do the rounds of the big houses in the district and perform their play in the hall or drawing room. At each they would collect gifts of cash or Christmas fare. So the rural poor had a strong incentive for keeping the plays alive.

Some of the mumming play costumes are traditional. In some instances, Victorian dress is used, but in most the characters are camouflaged by streamers and ribbons. In some the players are masked, while in some districts a tradition

33 Mummers in traditional costume of ribbons, Hampshire

survives, even where the performance of the play has long been discontinued, that the players should have their faces blackened. Apparently it was important that their everyday identity should be completely submerged in their roles in the drama, though in Sussex, where the mummers were known as 'Tipteerers', Jacqueline Simpson says, 'The general intention was to be as gay as possible, but neither to disguise oneself nor to "dress the part".'

The plays were most widely performed, or perhaps survived better, in the southern counties. Miss Simpson found evidence of them in no fewer than 45 towns and villages in Sussex. When conducting research for my book *The Folklore of Wiltshire* I was able to list 32 places with memories of mummers. Katharine Briggs has found 20 in Gloucestershire and 10 in Oxfordshire. There were at least ten in Devon, while in Hampshire almost every village had its mummers, some of them being still active. In about 1971 I was privileged to participate in a television programme with the New Forest Mummers (revived in 1967) who put on an extremely lively performance on a trestle-table in a country inn.

Christmas is the traditional season for the performance of mumming plays, Christmas Eve and the evening of Boxing Day being the most popular dates, but in some counties they are performed at other seasons. There is frequently a link between them and the Morris dancers.

Every race which has made its home in our islands has contributed to our Christmas customs. The mumming plays belong to the remote, probably pre-Roman era. The Romans themselves kept a week-long midwinter feast termed Saturnalia, when masters and men changed places and normal laws were suspended, — the probable origin of the 'Mischief Nights', to which frequent reference has been made. From the Saturnalia we inherit our custom of decorating our homes with evergreens.

Father Christmas's sleigh, drawn through the skies by reindeer, is Woden's chariot. Woden, the Norse god, used to hurtle across the sky at night, bearing gifts at this season for his faithful followers. When Woden was outlawed by Christian rulers, his place was taken by St Nicholas, whose feast-day was conveniently near. St Nicholas, too, was noted for giving presents and was, appropriately, the patron saint of children.

Perhaps it was a combination of one of the aspects of the Saturnalia (the switching of roles between master and men) and the association of St Nicholas with children that gave rise to the mediaeval custom, quite widespread, of appointing a boy bishop for the Christmas period. The boy was elected by his fellow choristers in the cathedral on St Nicholas's Day, 6 December, and held office till after Christmas. He was dressed in ecclesiastical splendour and performed all the duties of a bishop, except the celebration of Mass. The last event of his term of office was the conduct of a service on Holy Innocents' Day, 28 December, which commemorates the slaughter of the children of Bethlehem. If he died in office he was buried with all the honours due to a bishop, as is said to have happened at Salisbury, though historians have expressed doubts about an effigy in the cathedral there representing a boy bishop.

Another saint with a feast-day conveniently near Christmas is St Thomas, whose festival falls on 21 December. A widespread custom, which died out in most counties in the second half of the nineteenth century, as life became a little easier for the poor, was that of visiting houses in the neighbourhood to ask for alms. In some districts it was known as 'gooding' or 'goodening' but the more general term was 'Thomasing'. People spoke of 'going a-Thomasing', just as on the appropriate date in November they went 'a-Clementing'. In short, it was yet another excuse for house-to-house begging. On St Thomas's Day it was, in most places, confined to women and children, especially to widows, and the alms asked for were normally corn and milk, though money was gladly accepted. It was generally agreed that the corn was for baking the Christmas batch of bread or, in some places, for making frumenty. The custom was not thought of as begging, and was often indulged in by respectable people who would not have thought of asking for alms at any other season. Sometimes the women offered in return a sprig of holly or some other evergreen, as a token return for what was given. In many instances bequests stipulated that local charities should be distributed on St Thomas's Day, so that the recipients could enjoy the gifts at Christmas.

Similar in practice, though somewhat different in origin, was the custom of wassailing. The wassail bowl was a large bowl, traditionally made of maplewood though in special circumstances of silver, filled with a mixture of warming drinks. Ale or cider, often mulled (or heated), was the chief ingredient, to which were added spices, sugar, raisins, roasted apples, sliced oranges and any other pleasant ingredients available. It was, in fact, a kind of punch bowl. Wassail bowls were passed round at private parties and were also taken around villages by singers who asked for alms. The wassailing season was from Christmas Eve to Twelfth Night, culminating in the wassailing of the apple trees, described on pages 13-20. Traditional wassail songs are preserved in some parts of the country, and at Truro the wassailers still make their customary rounds.

To a large extent carol-singing has replaced wassailing. The object is the same, to collect money; and the carol-singers range from small children who stumble through one verse and then knock at the door to efficiently organised parties who trundle around a harmonium and perform for the benefit of the local church or some other charity. Carols were not originally confined to Christmas as they now preponderantly are; there were, for instance, Easter carols, some of which are found in modern church hymnals.

In her book *The Folklore of the Isle of Man* Margaret Killip has much about the traditional Manx carols, sung at Christmas Eve services known as *Oei'l Voirrey*. They were, she says, 'totally unlike English Christmas carols. A few were on the subject of the nativity . . . but in the main they were long rambling poems in the Manx language composed by the people themselves, many of them on the themes of sin and repentance, death and judgment, and the torments of hell'. Some of them were 30 or 40 verses long and were sung as solos, or by two singers taking alternate verses. After an hour or two spent in chanting these lugubrious sentiments it is understandable that the company should 'adjourn to the ale-

34 Carol Singers

house, to drink Manx home-brewed ale spiced with pepper, until the long Christmas candle had burned down in its socket'. Later the custom found its place in the calendar of the Methodist chapels, which played such a prominent part in the life of the island, though shorn of its ale-drinking and other less respectable aspects.

In a number of places, from Yorkshire to Hampshire, it used to be a custom to sing carols on Christmas morning from the top of a church tower.

The Christmas Candle, or Yule Candle, mentioned above, was once a common feature of the Christmas festivities. Placed on the table for the Christmas feast, it had not to be moved during the meal, nor blown out, nor snuffed out.

It had associations with the Yule Log, another obsolete feature, which used to burn on every hearth at Christmas. Both log and candle were lit at the same moment. The log was not brought into the house until Christmas Eve and, once lit, the fire was not allowed to go out until the log was entirely consumed.

In parts of Devon and Somerset an Ashen Faggot was substituted for the Yule Log. It consisted of a mass of ash twigs and small branches, bound together with as many withies as possible. As the withies snapped in the flames, so drinks were circulated or divinations practised. Sometimes each of the young people present chose a withy, and the order in which the withies burst would indicate the order in which they would marry. In other versions, the host called for a round of drinks each time a withy snapped. The faggots were often very large, as much as seven or eight feet long, and weighed a hundredweight or more. Smaller ashen faggots are still burned at Christmas in parts of the West Country.

Mistletoe, because of its pagan associations, was forbidden in most churches, with York Minster a notable exception. Mistletoe featured prominently in Norse mythology, as the plant by which the hero Baldur was slain. It was also a sacred plant in the old Celtic religion and was cut with much ceremony by the Druids. The practice of kissing under the mistletoe is very old, and in counties where mistletoe was scarce there was a tradition of making a 'kissing bush' of other evergreens and decorations, to be suspended from the ceiling.

Holly has usually been a permitted Christmas decoration, although it was in old times considered to be the home of woodland spirits and is sometimes, even now, regarded as a witches' tree. The belief that it is unlucky to bring holly into the house before Christmas Eve is widespread. Ivy is likewise an accepted evergreen.

Prince Albert, the husband of Queen Victoria, is usually given the credit for introducing Christmas trees to England, in 1847. Certainly from that time they quickly increased in popularity, but there are records of such trees in London streets in the Middle Ages.

A traditional Christmas dish used to be boar's head, the boar being a sacred animal to the primitive northern nations. In mediaeval times ordinary citizens generally feasted on roast beef or goose. Turkeys became popular soon after they were introduced in the sixteenth century. Christmas puddings, originally plum puddings, belong to a rather later period, but mince pies were certainly enjoyed in the reign of Elizabeth I. In Scotland and northern counties the Christmas meat was more likely to be mutton than beef, and there are references to haggis and giblet pie. The cereal dish, frumenty, was often served for breakfast, and poor neighbours or employees were invited in to share it.

Country folk used to believe firmly that bees sang in their hives on Christmas Eve and that oxen knelt in their stalls, their heads towards the east. In the Isle of Man sweet cicely, which the Manx people called 'myrrh', was said to blossom for a short hour on Christmas Eve. On Christmas Day the Glastonbury Thorn flowers, though some say it adheres to the original Christmas Day, 5 January. At any rate, it certainly flowers in midwinter. There are now other specimens of this subspecies of the common hawthorn, reputedly cuttings from the one at Glastonbury, at several places in Somerset, Herefordshire and elsewhere, including Clanville, in Hampshire. Cadnam, in the New Forest, has a celebrated oak which is said to produce buds on Christmas Day.

After the family feasting of Christmas Day, Boxing Day was held to be a day for outdoor sports, such as hunting and shooting, a custom which still holds. Small birds, which at other seasons would be considered not worth killing, were often shot, and, when squirrels were abundant, squirrel-hunting, or 'scuggy-hunting', was a popular sport. The shooting of birds was probably derived from the ancient practice of Hunting the Wren on St Stephen's Day, once widely observed throughout England and in the Isle of Man, Wales and parts of Ireland and Scotland. Edward A. Armstrong, in *The Folklore of Birds,* concludes that it derives from a very ancient Wren Cult which was carried by megalith builders and reached Britain during the Bronze Age. The wren was a sacred totem bird, slain and brought to life again, as happened to the hero in the mumming plays, as an analogy of the triumph of light over darkness.

St Stephen's Day was also the traditional date for 'blooding' horses, as noted in Chapter 2. Its alternative name of Boxing Day seems to have been derived from the one-time practice of putting contributions into a kind of earthenware 'piggy-bank' — a box which had to be smashed to get the money out, which was done on St Stephen's Day. The 'boxes' were originally given to servants and employees and later to anyone who had been of service during the year. Still later, children and paupers took to visiting the houses of local citizens and asking for alms, as on so many other occasions.

In Orkney and Shetland Christmas was still known as Yule until quite recent times, and, as is well known, throughout most of Scotland the festival is kept up with less enthusiasm than Hogmanay, New Year's Eve. The name Hogmanay is of unknown derivation but was in Northumberland applied to a small cake specially made for the festival. Most of the old Christmas customs observed in England are found associated with Hogmanay in Scotland, with the addition of others concerned with the day's significance as the threshold of the year.

In the Scottish Highlands a procession around a village or township was led by a man wrapped in a cow's hide, his followers beating the hide as a drum. It wound its way three times, sunwise, around each house, knocking on the walls while Hogmanay rhymes were chanted. The party was, of course, invited in and given refreshments, including whisky. Anne Ross, in *The Folklore of the Scottish Highlands,* records that the head of the household was presented with a *caisean-ucha,* — a stick around which part of the skin of a sheep, goat or deer had been wrapped. This was 'singed in the fire and carried three times sunwise round the family, grasped in the right hand and held to the nose of each person'. If a slice of the Christmas Cheese was preserved it possessed magical qualities of value in the coming year. For example, anyone lost in the mist on the hills had only to peer through a hole in the cheese to see where he was.

The hearth fire had on no account to be allowed to go out on New Year's Eve, or bad luck would follow. Incantations were said when the fire was banked up for the night. On New Year's morning great importance was attached to the 'first-footer', that is, the first person to set foot over the threshold. Ideally he should be a dark-haired man; it should certainly not be a woman. Nothing had to be removed from the house on New Year's Day, and to take fire to a neighbour who had been feckless enough to let her fire be extinguished was most unlucky.

'First-footer' superstitions were also common in England and Wales. Jacqueline Simpson, in *The Folklore of the Welsh Border,* says that the belief that the first visitor should not be a woman was very strong and still is. 'It must be a man or boy, preferably dark-haired. In Cheshire it was added that he must not squint, nor be flat-footed, nor have his eyebrows joining over his nose, and that he must silently lay gifts of bread and whisky on the table, and a coal on the fire; he would then be given wine and cake and would wish everyone in the house a Happy New Year.'

Superstitions regarding the 'letting-in' of the New Year are found in almost every county, and everywhere the good luck that attends a dark-haired man and the ill luck that is associated with a woman were believed in. In many instances a dark-haired man or boy was hired to be the 'first-footer'. There was a strong prejudice against red-haired men, though the situation was reversed in parts of Lincolnshire and Yorkshire, where fair-haired and red-haired men were considered lucky. The first water drawn from a well on New Year's Day was held to have magical qualities, helpful to both the general health and the complexion. In some places, as the 'first-footer' entered at the front door the back door had to be open, to let the Old Year out. Naturally, children made the most of the festival to visit houses asking for gifts. In the Welsh border counties they used to parade with apples in an attractive setting of leaves and tinsel, which they showed in return for a present of apples, sweets, mince-pies or cash. In the Exmoor district the children who went around singing and asking for money on New Year's Day had their faces blackened, presumably in accordance with the tradition that a black man must be the first-footer.

Superstitions regarding good luck and bad luck in the Christmas/New Year period are too numerous even to mention, but it was widely believed that one of the luckiest of persons was he or she who was born on Christmas Day. Among other gifts would be the ability to see spirits.

'Burning the Bush' was a ceremony frequently practised on farms in

Herefordshire and Radnorshire very early on New Year's Day until well into the nineteenth century. The bush, an old and dry hawthorn, was burnt on a wheat-stubble field, to protect the crops against evil spirits in the coming year. Sometimes the bush was soaked in cider, which makes the ceremony similar to some extent to the wassailing of apple trees. In Herefordshire, too, mistletoe cut on New Year's Eve was hung in the house as the clock struck midnight and stayed there for a year, when it was taken down and burnt.

Weather lore is also embarrassingly abundant. The saying, 'Green Christmas, full churchyard' is still well known. When Christmas Day falls on a Saturday it will be followed by a foggy winter and a cold summer. Much rain in the Christmas period will be followed by a wet year. If Christmas Day is a Sunday or a Monday, the following year will be windy. It is most important to see the first new moon of the New Year. In addition to turning the money in your pocket you should throw nine kisses to it and, if you are a woman, curtsey to it nine times. The unknown paths of the year ahead are so fraught with danger that you cannot be too careful.

Index